The
Numerology
Bible

The
Numerology
Bible

Teresa Moorey

The definitive guide to the power of numbers

FIREFLY BOOKS

A FIREFLY BOOK

Published by Firefly Books Ltd. 2012

First printing

Publisher Cataloging-in-Publication Data (U.S.)

A CIP record of this book is available from Library of
Congress

**Library and Archives Canada Cataloguing in
Publication**

A CIP record of this book is available from Library and
Archives Canada

Published in the United States by Firefly Books (U.S.)
Inc. P.O. Box 1338, Ellicott Station, Buffalo, New
York 14205

Published in Canada by Firefly Books Ltd.
66 Leek Crescent, Richmond Hill, Ontario L4B 1H1

Printed in China

Photo Credits
Clockwise from top left (All images from Shutterstock
Images): Login; Alexey Filatov; wisiel; KUCO; file404;
Michaela Stejskalova; Vudhikrai; Jag_cz; agsandrew

Contents

Introduction

'Number is the ruler of types and ideas and is the
cause of the Divine and angelic progressions'
(Pythagoras)

Numerology can give you extra insight into so many areas of your life. Confused about relationships? Numerology can help you to understand your true needs and find fulfilment. Lost your way career-wise? Your numbers can reveal your talents and empower you with new ideas.

Numerology is based on the premise that numbers express not only *quantity*, but also *quality*. This idea may be as old as civilization, and is enshrined in our language in respect of numbers 1 and 2 as *unity* and *duality*. The most ancient numerology tradition may be the Chaldean, dating from before the dawn of history. Numerology has been practised in various forms all over the world, from India and China to South America. It is found in systems such as the I Ching, the Tarot and the Hebrew Qabalah, which are discussed later, on pages 78, 86 and 92 respectively. Ideas about numbers evolve according to the prevailing culture, and it is right that they should. The intrinsic meanings of the numbers are esoteric

and eternal, but their manifestations may change. Numerology is something we work with, to develop and understand – it is a wisdom teaching, not a doctrine.

Pythagoras of Samos was one of the earliest known numerologists. Born around 600 BCE, he taught mysticism and philosophy to seekers who came from far and wide to benefit from his wisdom. He believed that numbers were sacred because they existed independently of material form. There is some evidence the Buddha may have studied with him, and together the two masters may have spread the teachings eastwards. Later, in the 5th century BCE, the Greek philosopher Plato recorded the insights of Pythagoras for posterity. We may speculate about how much numerology influenced the development of systems such as I Ching and Qabalah, but the truth is lost in the mists of time.

Pythagorus was a mysticist as well as a mathematician.

A basic tenet of Pythagoreanism held that the Universe was an expression of mathematical relationships. The Universe is vibration, and music is audible vibration. Pythagoras found that music is governed by numbers and that the pitch of a note is determined by the length of the string producing it. Harmonies thus depend on different wavelengths, and can be expressed as ratios or numbers. Numbers also underlie nature in respect of geometric proportions, with similar patterns repeating in seashells, flowers and planetary orbits. This is scientific fact, but it has also formed the basis of esoteric thinking throughout history. Patterning and cycles, harmonies and proportions are to be found in many subjects, from astrology to Feng Shui, as we shall see.

Early humans would have needed only a few numbers to keep account of their lives, and indeed even today some indigenous people can only count up to 2 – beyond that they just perceive 'many'. Numerology developed with civilization. It is encoded in Egyptian hieroglyphics, and the Pyramids were built using numerological measurements and symmetry. Great monuments have a numerological element; for instance, at Stonehenge

Patterns in nature reveal the mysterious powers of numbers.

in England there are 56 pits known as 'Aubrey holes' – the 5 plus the 6 add up to the Master Number 11, with its powerful influence on collective inspiration.

Numerology as we know it has evolved and adapted slowly since Pythagoras. In the 19th century, discoveries about light and magnetism made popular the theory that numbers related to energy patterns. Early in the 20th century, the writer Sepharial explored the links between numerology and astrology, names and the properties of nature. He made successful predictions for the stock market and horse races with numerology.

Some esotericists have also used Hebrew numerology, in which the numbers 1 to 12 are significant. The number 12 may be regarded as sacred because 4 (the basis of earthly life and the Four Elements) multiplied by 3 (the creative number of the Holy Trinity) makes 12. There are 12 signs of the zodiac, 12 numbers on the clock face, and so on. However, for modern Western culture, which uses nine digits, it is appropriate to use nine basic vibrational signatures, and this is the system employed by present-day numerologists.

One of the factors that affects numerology is human life expectancy. It used to be comparatively rare for people to reach

their allotted 'three score and ten' years, ie 70. Seven decades signified completion and many numerologists paid great attention to a system that covered

Previous page: Stonehenge was constructed according to numerological patterns.

Below: Hieroglyphics enshrine the meaning of numbers.

1 to 7. Now, with an increasing number of people living well beyond 80, the number 9 seems more important, and this is another factor in the use of nine types.

Numbers are all around us, and if you become aware of them you will soon find that patterns take shape. Maybe a certain number turns up for you more frequently than others. It is easy to get the

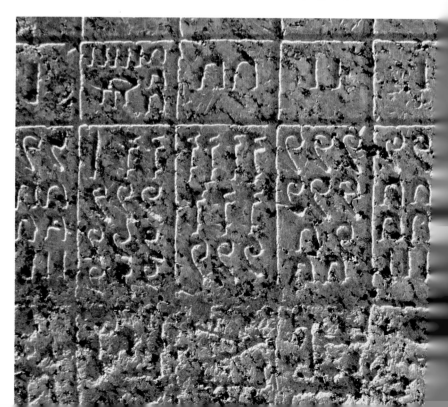

impression that numbers have a quality, a meaning, and then to wonder what that meaning may be. As you proceed through this book you will become familiar with the characteristics of the numbers. While you are dealing with something time-honoured that has inspired mystics and seers for millennia, your interaction with the numbers is part of your very own spiritual journey. This book is about exploring the significance of many numbers, from your birth date to your telephone number. Numbers also attach to your name, because your name is a vibration, and numbers are the language of vibration. In ancient times the letters in an alphabet also signified numbers while today our alphabet exists independently of numbers. Your name can be converted to numbers using the following table. The numbers are added up and converted to a single digit, as explained on page 101.

1	2	3	4	5	6	7	8	9
A	B	C	D	E	F	G	H	I
J	K	L	M	N	O	P	Q	R
S	T	U	V	W	X	Y	Z	

The Hebrew alphabet equated with numbers, and some numerologists convert this to our alphabet and use it to interpret names. You may like to experiment with the Hebrew letter values below – where the number 9 is not used.

1	2	3	4	5	6	7	8
A	B	C	D	E	U	O	F
I	K	G	M	H	V	Z	P
Q	R	L	T	N	W		
J		S			X		
Y							

Using This Book

If you have a specific problem or just feel that life has gone stale, consult your numbers for some inspiration and use this book as a guide to finding your way through the numbers that affect every part of your life.

This is not a book to be read from cover to cover. Dip into it when you need a little inspiration and insight and let the numbers speak to your intuition as they have spoken to many through the centuries. You are entering territory that has been trodden by mystics and sages down the ages. Our modern way is more light-hearted, but numerology can deepen your awareness, as well as making you contented and effectual.

The first chapter covers the basic characteristics of the numbers 1 to 9 and their manifestations. In chapter 2 you can discover how numerology links with other systems such as Tarot and astrology. Chapter 3 covers the five numbers, or *Five Formulas*, that apply to you. These will reveal what you are like, and give some hints about self-development, making changes and being positive: the numbers don't force you – they give you inclinations and choices. Visualizations can help your subconscious attune to the numbers, and your Five Formulas can help you with

relationships and lifestyle. In addition, you can gain a greater understanding about what is going on in your life at the moment by investigating your personal cycles. You may like to work out your Five Formulas, and also those of your family and friends, keeping these by you while you read the interpretations – there are spaces in the back of the book to record important numbers.

Chapter 4 covers correspondences – these are elements in the natural world that resonate with the numbers and can help you attune. Other important numbers are covered in Chapter 5, and Chapter 6 gives you insight into your relationships. In addition, you can gain a greater understanding about what is going on in your life at the moment by investigating your personal cycles in Chapter 7. Finally, Chapter 8 looks at everyday numbers in your life. Make a note of your telephone number, house number and any other important number like your car number, as these are relevant here.

Once you have worked out your numbers, read more about them in chapter 1.

Learn about the different formulas in chapter 3 and numerological relationships in chapter 6

chapters 7 and 8 will show you more about numbers in your life

Number 11

Introduction to the Formulas

Year 9

1: The Numbers

This chapter gives a general, cultural and spiritual description of the numbers, according to Western thinking. More specific details for each are provided in the 'Five Formulas' chapter (see page 96).

The Nine Frequencies of Life

In numerology we consider nine principal numbers, or 'vibrations', that make up the language of existence. These numbers are believed to represent all the different possible types of material manifestation, which combine and interrelate to form an individual. Although there are only nine 'types', you will have a variety of numbers occurring within your personality and your life. While you will share some of these with other people – for instance, several of your friends may have the same Life Path Number – there will be others that differ. Your numbers can show you where you have points of contact (or conflict), but you are always unique. See page 13 for more information on working out your numbers.

Why 9 numbers?

As you will see when you consider the section on Number 9 (see pages 56–9), there are several reasons for considering 9 as the number of finality and transition. So with 10 we begin a new cycle, with 10 reducing to 1 when 1 is added to 0. In the Pythagorean system, however, the numbers up to 10 are the essential numbers, and there are 10 Sephiroth on the Qabalistic Tree of Life (see page 95). This would suggest that 10, not 9, should be the defining number and that there may be 10 principal vibrations. It is also important to be aware that in our culture we make the transition to two digits at 10, but not all systems do – Roman numerals, for instance, do not. There is, nevertheless, a logic to the use of nine numbers.

When we reach 10 we have entered a new phase of creation, because 10 forms a totality and a new beginning. Human beings have 10 fingers, and these 10 fingers carry the initiative and enterprise of One. The Tree of Life has 10 Sephiroth, depicting a transition from pure spirit to earthly manifestation, or a journey from the material to the celestial. This is supposed to represent a complete picture of the Universe – which is a Unity. By contrast, the numbers 1 to 9 are about the manifestations encountered on earth.

In a sense, however, we do consider 10 essences, for the number 0 has also to be taken into account. In the Qabalistic Tree of Life the first Sephirah, Kether, may be regarded as the Great

Unknown, belonging to our Cosmos but not contained in it. A case may be made for equating this with 0, not 1.

In the end, however, with numerology as with all esoteric systems, it may be best to go with what fits our time and culture, for this is what forms the environment and the influences we attract. For many centuries we have used a system of single digits, 1 to 9, and this is deeply embedded in our subconscious. I believe it is important to use what we learn as an aid to intuition rather than as a closely defined and inflexible set of rules. Study the numbers and let your own experience guide you as you build up your store of wisdom.

Numbers are included in all we do and shape our lives.

Number 0

Zero is eternity, unbounded and endless, and it is also nothingness. Its glyph, the circle, suggests infinity, for the circle has no beginning and no end. However, it also conveys restriction – being 'encircled' leaves no room for choice or movement. Zero can also mean destruction, as in being reduced to nothingness. So Zero is a paradox. It refers to the unimaginably tiny, the atom with its circulating electrons, and the utterly boundless, which is the Universe, all possible universes and the unknowable beyond.

We don't work with Zero in the same way as we do with the other numbers, but it is helpful to remember that all flows from it and towards it. It is the melting pot of memories and of future creation. It forms the unknowable juncture where one cycle ends and another begins. Zero is also an eye that looks forwards and backwards, seeing all but able to influence nothing. Nor would Zero wish to influence anything – it is not impotent, but neither is it potent. It exists outside time and space and is not subject to cause and effect. It simply is.

Zero is not much used in numerology. It does not have a specific vibration because it is all vibrations and no vibration at all. However, Zero does have value to us as individuals and as a collective. The essence of Zero is the goal of many forms of meditation, and working with this symbol can refine your reflective powers. Entering the Lens of Zero from time to time enables you to withdraw and evaluate where you are in preparation for a fresh initiative. Zero reminds you that you are faced with completion and infinite possibility.

Zero cannot occur in your name, for all the letters have numerical values. However, it may be present in your Personality or Life Path Number. If you were born on the 10th, 20th or 30th of the month, or during the 10th month (October), then Zero is part of your make-up. This will also be the case with babies born in the 21st century, as with anyone

Zero is no number, yet it supports the meanings of other numbers.

born in the first decade of the 20th century, and at the completion of each decade, eg 1920 or 1930. If this applies to you, then from time to time you may be aware of the need to lose your form, to take a step back from the world and let go of identity, at least for a while. Using this consciously may help you. In fact, whatever your numerological composition may be, meditating on Zero can be freeing and renewing.

The challenges of Zero:

- What is the nature of infinity?
- Is it possible for there to be absolute nothingness?
- Contemplating Zero can lead to an altered state of consciousness that can bring about revelation.
- What may it mean to see through the eye of Zero and beyond?
- In the space symbolized by Zero all things are possible – what would you like to create?

The Greenwich Meridian in London indicates the point from which time can be measured.

Number 1

One relates to beginnings, potentials and initiative. It is the first step into the pregnant void, where all may be possible yet nothing has yet taken form. One brings with it courage, energy and positivity but, although it carries the impetus towards actualization, it is not so much about concrete achievement as the creation of opportunity. It is left to other numbers to flesh things out and earth them. One is the flash of inspiration, the pure urge to action.

Wherever One appears, something is coming into being – whether this will be something lasting and useful or just a lot of hot air depends on many factors, but One is always a force to be reckoned with.

If One is strong in your make-up, you are sure to be a pioneer in one respect or another. You will be ambitious, although this may not necessarily involve goals that others would recognize or value. Possibly you are a leader – people may follow you because you seem sure of your direction, single-minded and determined. However, it is unlikely that you seek to have influence over others – you just need to do your own thing. Like it or not, Number One is driven to break new ground, zooming like Superman out into space, motivated by a purpose that may be very hard to define. One may give the impression of tremendous strength and independence, and indeed this is often the case. No one struts their stuff with greater aplomb than One, at its best, full of confidence and assurance. However, it is also possible for Number One to experience great loneliness and isolation. If things go wrong, fear – even panic – can cause this trail-blazer to become rooted to the spot, feeling awkward and conspicuous. It is very important for Number One to have faith in themselves, in life and in the realm of possibilities, because without the impetus of One nothing can ever come into being.

Strong and indivisible, one confers single-mindedness and a unique approach.

Positive traits:

- Dynamism and initiative
- Independence
- Positive outlook
- Originality and uniqueness
- Courage
- Leadership

Challenges:

- Self-absorption – open your eyes and look around you
- Feeling solitary and misunderstood
- Secret fears about self-worth – don't demand quite so much of yourself
- Arrogance and pride
- Impatience and wilfulness
- Single-mindedness bordering on obsession

A strong sense of self, associated with One, does not have to mean selfishness.

Number 2

After the impetus of One comes the balance of Two. No creation has form until it is observed, no action has effect until there is a reaction. In essence, Two represents the first stirrings of self-awareness, and the awareness of the Other as a reality. Two is about relationships, about becoming truly conscious of something that is apart from oneself, about seeing contrasts and creating equilibrium.

This number is about companionship, but it is also about conflict, because it takes two to have a fight. Two is also the next step on the path to creation, signifying lover and beloved, artist and muse, builder and tools.

With Two featuring in your character you are always faced with the alternative, the other point of view, and you are likely to be conciliatory and sensitive. This number pours oil on troubled waters and may appear to be selfless at times, but this is because Two identifies with the other person so they almost *become* them. Relationships come first, last and in the middle, and Two seeks never to be alone. However, this number is also associated with separation, and sometimes the very thing Two fears most can come about, possibly because Two has lost their own identity and left the other party with little to relate to. Two is a conciliatory number, but surprisingly there may be a strong grain of dogmatism, because to a Two things may be black and white, right or wrong; so while this is the number of the peacemaker, it can paradoxically also signify the partisan – the person who perceives the opposites and feels bound to sign up for one side or the other.

Two is the gateway to the emotions, because as we relate to a 'significant other', who may be parent, lover, friend or business partner, we start to experience a whole range of feelings, from joy and fulfilment through disappointment, trauma and depression. Two can be overly passive, perhaps blaming others for what happens, but is also capable of giving and receiving immense happiness.

Two is about company, contrast, balance and also mirroring.

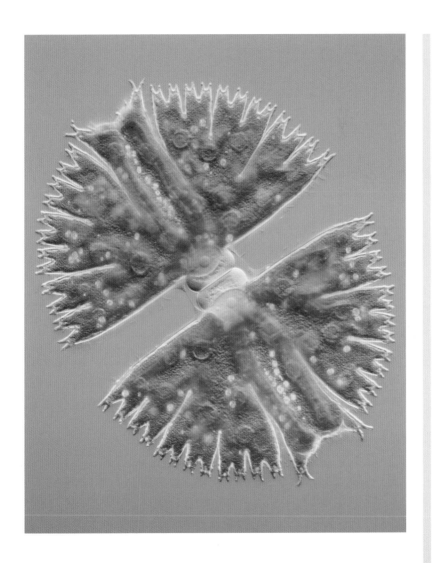

Positive traits:

- Cooperative
- Considerate
- Charming and diplomatic
- Kind and loving
- Sensitive
- Full of feeling

Challenges:

- Easily hurt – develop a thick skin
- Over-dependent
- Shy
- Critical – button your lip unless you have something nice to say
- Acting like a doormat
- Playing the martyr

Togetherness does not have to mean loss of identity. Two is company as they say.

Number 3

With Number Three we take a creative step towards the generation of new form. Three takes us from the single-dimensional realms of the point (One) and the line (Two) into the two-dimensional form of the triangle. Three relates to mother, father and child. Many important concepts arrange themselves into three elements: past, present and future; the three dimensions of space; force, matter and consciousness.

Three relates to awareness, because observer and observed are connected by observation, ie the ability to reflect. So Three is about generation, communication and also about playfulness, because it is through play that we learn best, as every child will demonstrate.

If Three is strong in your make-up, the chances are that you approach life joyfully, with a sense of potential. In all ways it will be important to Three to be expressive. Life is for living and this number may not take things too seriously – unless Three gets on a downer when it seems as if everything has been tried, and all that is left is disappointment or boredom. This is unlikely to last long, however, because Three soon finds something new to explore, or to fashion. With a strong Three, you tend to throw yourself into life – anything is worth at least one try, and you may be on the go all day, every day, determined not to miss anything. Three is a great multi-tasker – doing things one at a time may seem like a waste. Optimistic and positive, Three takes most events in their stride, often seeming lucky because they know how to go with the flow, grabbing chances when they arise and making the best of things. Flexible and spontaneous, Three is a 'happening' sort of person, but they can take on too much; if you are very 'Three', you must be careful that you don't suddenly realize that you have achieved little of real value, because important things may slip through your fingers if you are too casual.

Three creates abundance, laughter and confidence. But Three can also relate to loss, scattered energies and excess, as in 'Three's a crowd'. It is important for Three to focus and discriminate, to make their efforts count.

The creativity of Three is well-represented by the typical family.

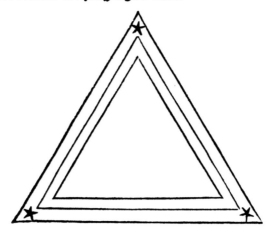

Eltoton autē vt in triangulū defo:mat̄:eqnis quo/ dāmō laterib⁹ ouobus: vno breuiore fed ppe ę ꝗuali reliquis: Inter eſtiuū ꝛ eqinoctialē circulū ſupꝛa caput arietis:nō longe ab andromedę oextro crure ꝛ perſei manu ſiniſtra collocatū: Cū ariete toto oc/ cidens. Exoriens autem cum eiuſdē oimidia pꝛioꝛe parte. babet autem ſtellam:in vnoquoqꝫ angulo vnam.

Triangulus

Unc pꝛotinus onodecim ſignoꝛū figurationē oice/ mus. Quoꝛū eſt pꝛinceps Aries in eqinoctiali cir/ culo conſiſtens: caput ad exoꝛtum babens euerſū: Occidens a pꝛimis pedibus ꝛ exoꝛiens: caput infra triangulū quod ſupꝛa diximꝰ tenens collocatū:pc/

- Creative
- Fun-loving
- Adaptable
- 'Ideas person'
- Expressive
- Sociable

Challenges:

- Wasteful – you will enjoy things more if you value them
- Too laid-back
- Superficial
- Extravagant – you can have too much of a good thing
- Trivial
- Immature

Groups of Three can have a dynamic and inspiring quallity. Goddesses are often grouped into three, such as the fates or graces.

Triangulation is used in architecture and astronomy to calculate distances between stars.

Number 4

With this number we enter the solid realms of the dimensions: length, breadth, height and time. Four relates to the ancient elements of Earth, Fire, Air and Water, and to the four states of matter: solid, liquid, gaseous and aflame. This is the number of stability, for tables and chairs need four legs to be steady.

Four appears in many of the systems by which we establish our place physically – there are four cardinal points to the compass, four seasons, and four points are needed to construct the simplest of solids, the tetrahedron. With Four, the human being is firmly rooted in space and time.

Not surprisingly, Four is linked to practicality. If you have a lot of Four in your make-up you will be down-to-earth, hard-working and largely a creature of habit. Reliable and predictable, Four's word is their bond. Routine is a must, boundaries are important and usually observed to the letter, and achievement – although it may be slow – is concrete. Four takes life seriously and keeps their nose to the grindstone, except when the blues take over and Four feels like the whole world

Four is related to the material world and is in therefore grounded and solid.

rests on their shoulders. This is a dutiful number, but sometimes life can appear joyless. When times are hard, Four may cold-shoulder more cheerful souls and trudge off to be a 'couch potato'. It is very important for Four to lighten up at times, and to reflect on what life is all about and what they are really trying to achieve, for this number is a true builder and actualizer. Four can create security and safety, making the world a better place, but they need to remember that humans 'do not live by bread alone'.

Self-disciplined and hands-on, Four is expert at handling and fashioning things, from actual materials to the organization of life. Very aware of the evidence of their senses, the Four person also needs to be aware of the gifts of sensuousness. Then their connection with physical experience can bring them close to the sublime, and they will be able to experience and convey deep contentment.

Positive traits:

- Practical and effectual
- Dutiful – very aware of responsibilities and laws
- Patient and calm
- Reliable – a 'rock' to friends and family
- Systematic and organized
- Hard-working and goal-orientated

Challenges:

- Over-cautious, sometimes to the point of being fearful
- Inhibited and may appear emotionally cold
- Lacking imagination – open your mind
- Over-thrifty
- Controlling and strict – does it really matter?
- Can be a 'plodder'

Four can act as a sound basis for building upon dreams.

Number 5

Number Five takes us beyond the material plane and into the 'happening' realms of mind and spirit. In the Western esoteric tradition, Five relates to the 'fifth' element, which is ether. Ether flows around and within the four material elements, energizing, connecting and going further. This is symbolized by the pentagram, or five-pointed star, which is a potent magical symbol.

There are five elements in Chinese Feng Shui: Earth, Fire, Metal, Water and Wood. This system relates to different 'energies' and includes the concept of chi or life force (see page 80), which is synonymous with *prana* and *orgone*. So Five takes us into the realms of ideas, abstracts and mental constructs.

Five is linked to lots of movement, activity and communication. With a strong Five, you will have places to go, people to see and plenty of irons in the fire. Change is ever-present – getting stuck in a rut would be death to Five, but that rarely happens for Five does not stay still in one place long enough to be caught. There is a lot of vitality, and a huge potential to bring in the new and get things moving; but whether that actually sticks or slips away like quicksilver depends on Five focusing their considerable mentality and being stimulated enough to continue.

Five comes midway between One and Nine, and it is about *becoming*, journeying from what has been built with solid foundation by Four to the transcendence of Nine.

Restless, needing to know how things work and thirsty for experience, Five is adaptable and alert, easily excited and easily bored. However, this number does not seek to overthrow the status quo that Four has built. The urge in Five is to use their intelligence and analytical qualities for understanding structures and processes and to use their resourcefulness to make them work better. There is a tension in Five between tradition and freedom, for there is a place for both to be cleverly used. The same goes for emotion and intellect. Five has many alternatives – choosing well brings acumen and inspiration and can take the strongly five person into inspiring territory.

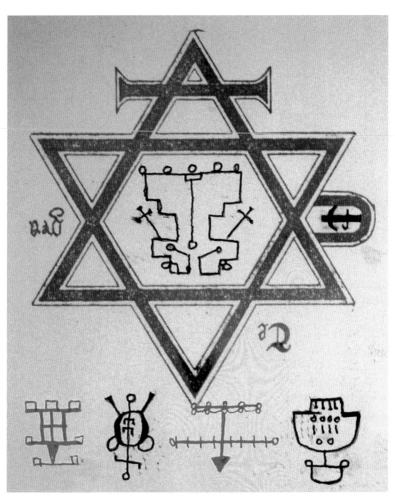

Five works in the realm of ideas and designs that can change consciousness.

Positive traits:

- Ingenuity and curiosity
- Adaptable
- Clever and analytical
- Lots of movement and variety
- Abundance of experience to learn from
- Free-spirited and adventurous

Challenges:

- May be unreliable
- Restless and 'on edge' – practise relaxation
- Irresponsible
- Lacking discipline and self-indulgent
- Short-sighted – use your observant qualities
- Rebellious and 'awkward'

The freedom craved by five can open mental doors.

Number 6

Six is the completion of the second cycle of three energies, bringing us to a point of fulfilment and consummation. Four built, and Five explored the structure that was created. Now Six wants to show off that structure, revelling in its attractiveness and comfort. Beauty, harmony and a sense of balance are vital.

The figure 6 is similar to the ancient form of the spiral, found on many prehistoric artefacts. This symbol means the passage into and out of manifestation, hinted at in the flowing form of Six. Three may have created, but Six is also concerned with the meaning of creation, wanting it to be a perfect expression of something absolute. The six-pointed star, or Star of Solomon, is a potent magical symbol composed of two interlocking triangles. The triangle that points downwards signifies the Great Feminine, while the triangle pointing upwards represents the Great Masculine – the interplay of spirit and matter. Together they are complete and symmetrical. The father-mother-child triad of Three is here, but Six is also about home and extended family.

If Six is strong in your nature, you are probably idealistic and beauty-loving. Wherever you go, you like to create lovely surroundings, to look your best and to spread a feeling of happiness and serenity. You have an idealistic vision that can lift you and others beyond the commonplace and you may be very intuitive, especially about people's situations. Your capacity for enjoying life is second to none and you are relaxing to be with. However, you may be a tad lazy, and even escapist. Your ideal world is not always actualized in life, and that can be very hard to take. Your way of entering it may be through books and films, but in worse scenarios a strong Six can predispose you to excess and addiction. In the Bible book Revelation, 666 is the Number of the Beast, indicating that too much Six energy can lead you astray, seeking gratification rather than spreading love, being seduced by the form rather than pursuing the essence. The better aspect is that Six can liberate the divine within, showing yourself and others the best 'me' you can be.

Six is aware of the beauty that exists all around and seeks to extend it.

The sense of community of six is deeply enriching.

Positive traits:

- Peace-loving and responsible
- Creator of beauty and all things pleasant
- Helpful and supportive
- Knows how to enjoy life
- Domestic goddess
- Wonderful sense of family

Challenges:

- Can be jealous – always count what you have
- Sometimes lazy and escapist
- Easily seduced – hold to your true values
- Smug and complacent
- Meddling and busybody
- Domestic tyrant

Number 7

Seven lifts us to a fresh level of understanding. The balance of Six takes on a new component, searching for completion; with Seven the natural begins to return to the spiritual, as the spiral of Six winds towards its source. There are seven days of the week, seven ages of Man, seven notes in the musical scale and seven colours in the visible spectrum.

Seven is also associated with the Moon because seven days are approximately one quarter of the Moon's cycle, from new back to new again. The Moon has long been linked to magic, for the intuition is often felt most powerfully when the Moon is full. So Seven is a magical number, relating to changes we may make in the world around us through the powers of our will and imagination.

If Seven features strongly in your make-up, you are likely to be dynamic, although this may not always be obvious. Not for you the single-mindedness of One, the never-say-die irrepressibility of Three or the frenetic pace of Five. You are more subtle, and sometimes secret. You may be interested in the link between matter and spirit and, if you are not literally exploring this, there will be something in your approach that looks for the hidden and seeks change at a deep level. Probably you have a magnetic, enigmatic air –

people don't always understand you, and they may find you spacey and absent-minded. In some way, you are on a quest to discover more about yourself. Your searches may take you into the realms of psychology and parapsychology, or you may be fascinated by the laws that govern the material world. You may seek knowledge for its own sake, knowing that knowledge is power, but you are also motivated by a desire to do good in the world. Sometimes it seems as if things just 'happen' around you – is this some strange ability that you possess, or have you set things in motion behind the scenes? Often the answer is not obvious.

Seven can be moody and even explosive at times – changes are going on within you, and the lessons of life are not always easy. You may become a tad obsessive

Seven looks beyond this world and can be spiritual and imaginative.

about proving yourself. However, whether on an inner level or an outer one, your accomplishments will be impressive and you are sure to 'make a difference'.

Positive traits:

- Wise and thoughtful
- Catalyst for galvanic change
- Refined and reserved
- Spiritual
- Stoical and strong-willed
- Brilliant analyst

Challenges:

- Scepticism – remember that the true sceptic has an open mind, and is not a determined disbeliever
- Fault-finding
- Aloof and unreachable – it is worth trying to explain yourself
- Lonely and isolated
- Pessimistic – remember to be positive because you will thereby create good things
- Devious – sometimes the direct route is the best

Eight is the ambitious number that builds on achievement.

Number 8

In some senses the number Eight has a dual meaning. On the one hand, it is the number of material power and success, made up as it is of the doubling of the highly practical Four. On the other hand, it follows Seven, which signifies the completion of experience in this world – so Eight potentially leads on to a new level.

There are eight orifices in the female body, and the Feminine is the gateway to life – so Eight may be a number of new life, and in many churches the font is an octagon. Eight may be the womb that is also the tomb; the power of the earth, first felt with Four, now takes on a more mystical significance.

The figure 8 placed on its side is the sign for infinity – Eight may be the number of the world to come, although of course that may mean reconnection with this world, if one believes in reincarnation. Eight has also been regarded as the number of Fate. Revelations gives 888 as the number of Christ. It has many links with Jewish belief – circumcision is practised eight days after birth, at the Feast of Dedication eight candles are burned, and the celebration lasts eight days. There were eight prophets descended from Rahab, eight sects of Pharisees, and Noah was the eighth in line of descent from Adam.

With a strong Eight you are likely to take life seriously, have a potent sense of destiny, and to regard existence as a set of challenges and obstacles to be overcome. You have the capacity for great success, but also for spectacular failure. Deep inside you possess the sense of being a servant to the cycle of life and death, yet you also have the will to wield your knowledge and ability to gain power and control. Ultimately we are all at the mercy of Fate – you know that. But sometimes it is as if you want to stave this off for as long as possible and grab as much sovereignty as you can. In all probability you will gain a position of some authority and stature; this will give you much satisfaction because it makes you feel you will be leaving something enduring behind you, and that you have bagged your slice of the eternal. If you understand that the finest qualities of a ruler are compassion and fairness, what you generate will deserve to last.

Positive traits:

- Great manager or director
- Authoritative
- Will to succeed
- Practical on a large scale
- Able to manage large sums of money
- Powerful presence
- Ambitious and entrepreneurial
- Sense of mission/destiny

Challenges:

- Possible misuse of power
- Machiavellian
- Irresponsibility with important resources
- Greedy – remember enough is as good as a feast
- Overly materialistic – you cannot take it with you
- Could be vengeful
- Neglect of material concerns – be careful not to lose focus
- Scheming – openness may get best results

Eight's sense of structure can lead to insight and power.

Number 9

Nine is a number of completion and transition. The first set of numbers has come to a culmination and there is both fulfilment and dissolution, as preparation is made for passage through the eye of infinity, Zero, before re-emerging into a new cycle. Three, the number of generation, has now been repeated three times – creation is complete.

Nine has several interesting properties. Mathematically, it is the only number that always reproduces itself when multiplied by another number: 5×9=45, 4+5=9; 6×9=54, 5+4=9 – this is the same with every number that it is multiplied by. Any number added to 9 will always reproduce itself: 1+9=10, 1+0=1; 2+9=11, 1+1=2; and so forth. If all the digits up to and including 9 are added together the sum total is 45, which reduces to 9.

With Nine there is a sense of returning to source. Christ died at the ninth hour, there are nine planets in the solar system (although there are arguments about the status of Pluto), and several groups of goddesses are nine in number, eg the nine muses. There are nine months in the average pregnancy (this is more accurately nine lunations). A total of 360 degrees makes a complete circle, and 360 reduces to 9. If Nine features in your personality, you will have an urge to move

beyond, to experience more and to push back boundaries. You have big ideas and want to take the world in an embrace, but individuals may not appeal so much and despite your charm there is a detachment about you and a sense of the Otherworld. You may be very unselfish, but you may also be quite egotistical as you strive to earth those fantastic notions of yours. You may know many things and want to teach others about them – it is important for you to serve humanity. However, your own emotions are also strong and you may be quite wild and passionate. People may regard your ideas as quirky or unconventional. For your part, you cannot be bothered with anything boring, and that will include small-minded individuals. With a strong Nine, freedom and adventure are essential to you, but above all you seek spiritual meaning and may want to 'justify the ways of God to men' – no small task, but you are up for the task.

The idealism of nine takes in a broad vision of humanity.

Nine is far-seeing and may be bored by petty details.

Positive traits:

- Humanitarian and charitable
- Romantic and imaginative
- Able to put your personal interests last
- Great charm and charisma
- Deep compassion
- Gifts as a teacher and mentor
- Compassionate and philanthropic
- Adventurous – pushes back boundaries

Challenges:

- Sometimes egocentric
- You can go to extremes
- Occasionally you have ulterior motives and believe the end justifies the means
- You can be vain and self-glorifying – modesty will get you more respect
- Prejudice and dogma may creep in where you least expect – beware of tyrannical liberalism
- Sometimes you switch off your compassion
- Unconsciously you may fall into pettiness
- You may be antisocial

Master Numbers

Although the nine basic 'types' from One to Nine are of paramount importance, there are certain numbers that are considered to be *Master Numbers*. These numbers are 11, 22, 33 and 44. Any double-digit number may be considered a Master Number, but meanings become extremely refined. Besides, after 44 the digits have to be added more than once to reduce to a single digit – e.g. 55=5+5=10, 1+0=1. For practical purposes, only 11 and 22 are very important, because the days of the month only go up to 31, making it impossible to have 33 as a Personality Number.

Some numerologists are very impressed by numbers 11 and 22, regarding them as exceptional and distinct from the 2 and the 4 to which they reduce. However, the truth of the matter is that these Master Numbers are not especially rare. On the journey of reducing a name or a date to a 2, 11 will usually be the number arrived at before the final stage, because 2 only results from 1+1, or 2+0. The only exception to the 11 stage is where a date or name adds up to exactly 20 – otherwise 20 is always bypassed because no two digits alone are ever going to have it as their sum. The last date in the 20th century when that would have been possible was 1.1.1980, although in the 21st century it is more common.

Your Here-and-Now Number (see pages 104-205)may add up to 20, as may your Soul Number, but it is unusual to have a name that is short enough for a Destiny Number to make 20 – so 11 is more usually the final stage before 2. The case for 22 is somewhat similar, although 13 is also a frequent precursor to a final 4.

It is important to keep 11 and 22 in perspective, but if they turn up in your formulas you have a choice. Will you respond to the higher demands of these numbers or concentrate on more mundane matters? The Master Numbers may be more demanding, but they are potentially more fulfilling.

Responding to the vibration of 11 can bring out your best.

Number 11

Eleven has great resonance because the pair of Ones that compose it magnify each other, giving power and purpose to the basic Two. With a strong Eleven you may be able to channel messages from the subtle planes. This does not mean that you will be a medium or 'channeller' as such – in fact you may be sceptical about such things. However, your Eleven gives you a special type of inspiration that can be of great benefit to other people and maybe to the world at large.

The basic receptivity and intuition of Two means that understanding may be non-verbal, but with Eleven there may be the ability to find words to motivate and enthuse.

for a personal closeness but for humanity itself. This could result in a loss of identity, as the Eleven person is possessed by a vision. If Eleven is your number, you will need a powerful dose of objectivity in

Eleven has been called the number of the prophet, or Messiah. The partnerships that are so vital to Two are here carried to the next level so that the relationship may be to large groups of people, and sacrifice made not necessarily

An eleven person may involve you in issues that transcend the personal.

order to make it work for you, along with the willingness to examine yourself critically, but positively – depression may be possible with Eleven, if the ideals lose their meaning.

Eleven is the number of the faithful apostles of Jesus – the 12th was Judas, who betrayed him. Eleven may be seen as the light of revelation, shining into the mundane world. There are 10 Sephiroth on the Qabalistic Tree of Life, with 10 therefore representing manifest existence, and 11 the power above and beyond. We speak of the '11th hour' as being the very last opportunity to achieve anything. Eleven has also been described as the number of balance. It equates with Justice in the Tarot pack, and the sign for Eleven, two parallel lines, implies two equal forces working in tandem. It may also be seen as the doubling of the potency of Number One, by adding an equal, complementary force – thus it may represent the balance of male and female, yin and yang. However, it is important to remember that 11 is the glyph we use in the modern Western world and this is not universally employed. This could mean that such interpretations are very specific to our culture.

If Eleven is your number, or if you choose to respond to the Eleven 'vibration', make sure that you 'saint' yourself in moderation, balancing conviction with humility, inspiration with realism, and you will be amazing.

Positive traits:

- Visionary
- Self-sacrificing
- Unselfish zeal
- Psychic
- Revealing new perspectives
- Spiritual
- Artistic talents
- Charisma

Challenges:

- May be fanatical
- Highly strung
- Not always honest – you may tell yourself the facts don't matter
- You may have a superiority/inferiority complex
- Watch out you don't disappear into fantasy
- You may say things just to get attention
- Your ego could become inflated – remember you are only human

Number 22

Like its summation, Four, Twenty-Two is a builder – in fact this is the number of the master-builder. If you identify with Twenty-Two, then you want what you build to mean something. Extending from the Four's wish to construct a secure foundation for your life, and the lives of those you care for, you may want to create something that will stretch outside your personal orbit and even beyond your own lifetime.

The double Two influence brings sensitivity and compassion, and this may lift you out of the 'small-print zone' in which Four sometimes gets stuck, and into the wider sphere.

Twenty-Two is a number of esoteric significance. There are 22 paths on the Qabalistic Tree of Life, that take the spiritual explorer from one Sephirah to another. There are 22 cards in the Major Arcana of the Tarot – although these are

Twenty-two may be a powerful number that must be used with care.

numbered 0 to 21, adding to the mystery of Twenty-Two, because it is not the spoken number. There are 22 letters in the Hebrew alphabet, representing the 22 vibrations of the voice of God when the Universe was created. Twenty-Two has been a number chosen by prophets, magicians and philosophers to convey their ideas. For instance the Revelation of St John was written in 22 chapters, St Augustine wrote the *City of God* in 22 books, the occultist Eliphas Levi divided each volume of his *Doctrine and Ritual* into 22 chapters and Aleister Crowley, the magician, wrote *Magick in Theory and Practice* also in 22 chapters.

If Twenty-Two is strong in your make-up, then you are a true creator. You have deep feelings and you feel compelled to turn these into something concrete. It is not enough to lament the suffering in the world; you want to build a shelter for the homeless or an organization that will grapple practically with the issues involved. You may have a quiet and systematic approach to life, and if you are wise you will probably cultivate this. But one day you realize that you have brought something glorious into being. You have the potential for greatness – as a creator, teacher and organizer you can be immensely successful and admired universally. However, power itself is

neutral, and you can use your abilities to help the less fortunate, become a business tycoon or be a master criminal. Use it well!

Positive traits:

- Enlightened
- Pragmatic idealist
- Humanitarian
- Powerful in many spheres and on many levels
- Gets results
- May work globally
- Can be visionary and inventive

Challenges:

- Can be very stubborn and wilful
- Your rage can be highly intense
- Disillusionment can make you destructive
- You may live on your nerves
- You may want power for its own sake
- Sometimes you can be contrary, to avoid being 'ordinary'
- You could be tempted to do something criminal because you have no time for petty laws

Other Master Numbers

Meanings become more obscure and subtle the higher the master number so it is usually more useful to reduce numbers to a single digit. Here are two Master Numbers that you may find useful as part of the picture of life.

Number 33

You can see the overall picture and are deeply affected by the needs of others. Your double Three influence means you love to bring joy, and the total Six means you are very compassionate, but you may feel guilty at not giving enough, or giving too much. Be careful that your image of perfection is not an illusion, or you could get very depressed. Look for the sacred in life, but don't feel you have to live up to it. A good motto for you is 'It is better to light a candle than to curse the darkness'. If you can be content with this, you will know peace of mind.

Number 44

You are wonderful at laying down the foundations for others to build on and your instinct for survival is second to none. Responsible and thorough, you may sometimes get fed up with shouldering so much. Give yourself time to play, to laugh, and just to 'stand and stare'. This is very important; if you don't then all you achieve could seem to turn to dust as you lose the 'spark' and you may let everyone down, especially yourself.

The master numbers have numerological meanings that are key to their interpretation.

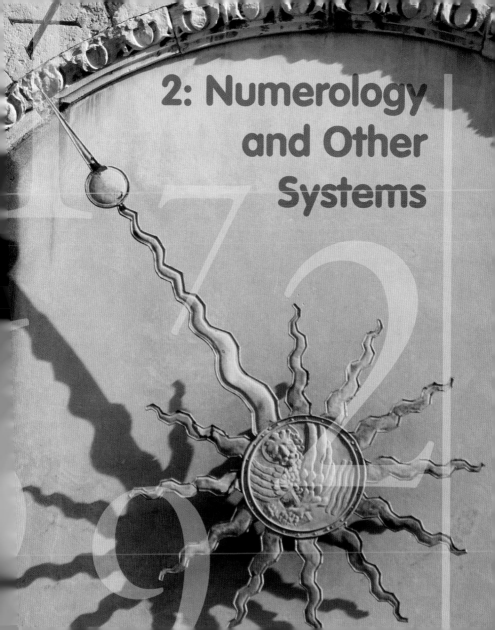

2: Numerology and Other Systems

Esoteric Numbers

There are many systems other than numerology that reflect the hidden meanings of life. It is tempting to expect these systems to dovetail. However, while there are many correspondences, there are also differences. So which way is the 'right' way?

The answer is that esoteric methods are an aid to your intuition and they don't have to 'match' or comply with the demands of logic. Other models of the hidden energies around us can link with numerology, but always go with what feels right and useful to you. These links will make more sense if you first read the 'Introduction to the Numbers' on pages 16–67. However, here is a very quick guide to the characteristics of the numbers, for reference:

1 initiating	**4** building	**7** deepening
2 balancing	**5** connecting	**8** empowering
3 creating	**6** harmonizing	**9** understanding

Astrology spells out the cycles of life and expresses the essence of each of the numbers as the wheel of life turns

At the centre of the I Ching lies the Yin and Yang – supreme symbol of cosmic balance.

Astrology and Numerology

In astrology there are 12 signs of the zodiac and 10 principal heavenly
bodies to take into account. There are also the aspects, or angles between
these bodies. These correlate with numerology in a variety of ways.

Signs of the Zodiac

1 ♈ Aries

This is the first sign of the zodiac, beginning at the spring equinox. Aries is about assertion and individuality and correlates obviously with 1. As the fourth sign in the calendar year, achievement and practicality are highlighted, but this is less obvious.

2 ♉ Taurus

Second in the zodiac, sensual and passive Taurus has links with 2. As the fifth sign in the calendar year, Taurus has the sexuality of 5 but usually lacks the changeability and the urge to communicate.

3 ♊ Gemini

Third in the zodiac. Lively and communicative, the cheerful 3 vibration to some extent fits Gemini. As the sixth sign in the calendar year, Gemini is a 'people person' and likes to cooperate, at least on the surface, although some of the 6 qualities such as love of home and beauty are not classical Gemini traits.

4 ♋ Cancer

Fourth in the zodiac. As a lover of stability and safety, 4 harmonizes with Cancer, but is incompatible with the sensitivity and imagination of the sign. Cancer is seventh in the calendar year and some of the mystery and 'privateness' of 7 are characteristic.

5 ♌ Leo

Fifth in the zodiac, Leo has the self-expressive qualities of 5, but not the unpredictable changeability. As eighth in the calendar year, Leo exhibits a will to power, but is not always as practical.

6 ♍ Virgo

Sixth in the zodiac, Virgo is helpful and perfectionist but less emotional than the 6 personality. Ninth in the calendar year, Virgo is changeable and adaptable but more prone to use logic and restraint than the 9 vibration might suggest.

7 ♎ Libra

Seventh in the zodiac, Libra shows some of the analytical qualities of 7, but the tact and charm of the sign are not necessarily reflected. As 10th in the calendar year, the 1 vibration influences Libra, and this sign can occasionally be stubborn and bossy.

8 ♏ Scorpio

Eighth in the zodiac, the will to power and achievement is often strong in Scorpio, although Scorpio is not always comfortable with overt leadership.

Each of the twelve signs has numerical links.

9, with the occasional trace of superiority. As 12th in the calendar year, the cheerfulness of 3 can break through.

10 ♑ Capricorn

As the 10th sign of the zodiac, Capricorn displays the solitary self-sufficiency of 1. This is reinforced by the fact Capricorn is first in the calendar year, bringing individuality and the willingness to meet challenges. However, Capricornian pragmatism may not be reflected.

11 ♒ Aquarius

The detachment of Aquarius may not resonate with its position as second in the calendar year, linking it with 2. However, Aquarius can be diplomatic and tolerant, putting itself last. As 11th sign of the zodiac, the 2 influence repeats – however, with Aquarius we see the working of the Master Number 11, which can bring high expectations and the wish to influence others spiritually.

12 ♓ Pisces

The 12th sign of the zodiac is also third in the calendar year, bringing a double 3 influence. Pisces is cheerful, generous and creative, and loves to bring joy to others, but it does not always exhibit the characteristic confidence of 3 and may be muddled and changeable.

As 11th sign in the calendar year, the 2 influence (see page 62) brings out the Scorpionic intuition.

9 ♐ Sagittarius

This ninth sign of the zodiac displays all the adventurous and generous qualities of

Numerology and the Planets

1 ☉ Sun

As primary light in the solar system, the number 1 characterizes the Sun. Although the Sun is a force for integration – the 1 personality does not always follow this.

2 ☽ Moon

Second of the luminaries, the Moon correlates with 2, the Eternal Feminine. Through its cycle and esoteric associations, eg qabalah, it links with 9.

3 ☿ Mercury

Planet of communication, 5 is the number that fits Mercury, but numerologists don't always agree and link it with 8 or 3.

Since time immemorial the planets have been numbered according to their distance from Earth.

4 ♀ Venus

The number 6 harmonizes with Venus, the love planet, although 2 and possibly 3 also have Venusian qualities.

5 ♂ Mars

Planet of assertion and aggression. The numbers 1 and 5 have Martian links. The crusader aspect of 9 has a little Mars.

6 ♃ Jupiter

Cheerful 3 is Jupiterian, and the expansiveness of 9 also reflects this planet.

7 ♄ Saturn

The numbers 8 and 4, the numbers of challenge and mastery, may link with Saturn, lord of discipline. Also 1, for Saturn can be solitary.

8 ♅ Uranus

Unpredictable 5 carries the rebellious Uranus vibe.

9 ♆ Neptune

This dreamy planet can be seen in the mysterious workings of 7 and possibly in the selflessness of 9, and empathy of 6.

10 ♇ Pluto

Transformative Pluto may be discerned in the urge to power of 8, but has also been linked to 0, the great void.

Astrological Aspects

Links between the signs of the zodiac and numbers are not neat or definite, and the same applies to the planets. However, it is with the *aspects*, ie the angles made by the planets, one to another, that numerology truly dovetails with astrology. The planets are plotted on the 360-degree circle of the birthchart, and form aspects with each other, determining how they will work together. According to many astrologers, these angular relationships reveal defining elements in the personality, and are also crucial in other forms of astrology, such as the divinatory *horary astrology*.

1 ☌ Conjunction

Planets are together and operate in unison, focused, intense and perhaps with little regard for the rest of the chart. People with strong conjunctions in their chart usually exhibit '1' characteristics.

2 ☍ Opposition

Planets are 180 degrees apart, dividing the sphere into 2. This can lead to balance or anxiety, indecisiveness and division. Also emphasized awareness of the other perspective or the other person, which is typical of 2.

3 △ Trine

Planets are 120 degrees apart, dividing the circle into 3. Considered a happy, flowing aspect, very creative, but may be prone to complacency and over-casualness, reflecting 3.

4 ☐ Square

Planets are 90 degrees apart, dividing the circle into 4. Challenging and often obstructive, squares require that we grapple with the world and they can be frustrating and/or constructive, as 4.

5 Q Quintile

Planets are 72 degrees apart, dividing the circle into 5. This relates to talents, knowledge and inventiveness, echoing the essence of 5.

6 ✶ Sextile

Planets are 60 degrees apart, dividing the circle into 6. This is the 'busy bee' aspect, of creative, repetitive action, reflecting the harmony and productivity of the 6 vibration.

7 1/7 Septile

Planets are 56 degrees 26 minutes apart. This is an uneasy relationship requiring questioning, creating an explorative unrest. It is the only number into which

360 cannot be divided exactly. This aspect is little used by astrologers and it reflects the inaccessibility and mystery of 7.

8 △ Semi-square

Planets are 45 degrees apart, dividing the circle into 8. It reflects purpose, productivity and a mastery that comes from challenges overcome – recognizably 8 in character.

9 1/9 Novile

Planets are 40 degrees apart, dividing the circle into 9. Joy and happiness result from understanding and can be spread to the outside world. Spirituality and mysticism are likely – all characteristic of 9. This aspect is little used by astrologers.

As time moves on, each number has its turn.

Numerology and the I Ching

The Chinese spiritual pathway called *Taoism* is one of the oldest on earth. This gave rise to the divination system called the I Ching, which is based on the relationship between the forces of *yin* and *yang*, and was inspired by the markings on a turtle shell.

The system was formalized by Confucius in the 6th century BCE. The I Ching is composed of lines, which are either broken or continuous. Continuous lines are yang; broken lines are yin. The combination of yin and yang is what gives a trigram (an arrangement of three lines)

its meaning. The eight trigrams occur in four natural pairs that complement each other. The qualities that we associate with the numbers 1 to 8 are mirrored in the I Ching interpretation. Numbers 4 and 8 have gentler and more positive interpretations in the I Ching. While our Western interpretations may be biased by our traditional lack of respect for the yin, or passive, female approach, Chinese interpretations offer more balance.

The I Ching is one of the most venerable and informative divination systems.

The Trigrams

The first pair consists of Heaven and Earth, yang and yin, being the source of life:

1 Chi'en – Heaven, Sky
Achievement. Creativity, logic, courage, focused energy, identity, assertiveness, success, confidence.

2 K'un – Earth
Acceptance. Receptivity, consideration, intuition, patience, docility, nurturing. Body: stomach, abdomen, womb.

The second pair refers to diffused energy, being Fire and Water (or The Abyss):

3 Li – Fire
Inspiration. Illumination, cleansing, clarity, communication, creativity.

4 K'an – Water, The Abyss
Feeling, tuning in to emotions, fearlessness, danger, hardship.

The third pair refers to movement:

5 Chen – Thunder
Regeneration, seeds of new life, arousal, surprise, spontaneity, male sexuality.

6 Sun – Wind, Wood
Persistence, gentle but determined progress, adaptability, flexibility, endurance, justice.

The fourth pair refers to stillness:

7 Ken – Mountain
Vision, stillness, withdrawal, silence, meditation, spirituality.

8 Tui – Lake
Secrecy, dreams, psychism, magic, pleasure, tranquillity, healing, consolidation.

Numerology and Feng Shui

The Chinese system of Feng Shui is based on the premise that the way articles are arranged in a building influences the subtle conditions at work, and can have far-reaching effects. The things we surround ourselves with are not merely 'things' – they have an essence, a symbolic quality, and they affect the flow of unseen energy, called *chi*.

Chi needs to move freely, but not in too hectic a fashion. Rooms need to be balanced with consideration for the 'vibrations' in specific areas. The concept of yin and yang underlies Feng Shui, but when applied properly it is a complex system. 'Feng Shui' means 'Wind, Water' and Feng Shui principles arise from the unseen powers of nature.

According to Feng Shui principles the space to be considered is divided into nine areas. These correspond to the eight directions of the compass and a central point. An octagonal diagram called the *Pa Kua* depicts this, showing eight equal segments with the ninth space at the centre sometimes displaying the yin/yang sign. The Pa Kua translates into the *Lo Shu*, or 'magic square', showing nine segments. Each segment is numbered in such a way that in whatever direction you add the numbers – up, down or diagonally – you arrive at the number 15.

This square is some of the oldest magic known. It appears in the Western tradition as the Saturn square – so called because Saturn is related to the third Sephirah on the Qabalistic Tree of Life, and this magic square contains *three* rows of *three* figures. Each of the nine segments in the Pa Kua, or Lo Shu, relates to an area of life, thereby providing a plan to assess the characteristics of the space and how it will affect the occupants. Segment One, at the bottom centre of the diagram, relates to success and career, appearing in the north. To its left, in the north-east, is Segment Eight, relating to knowledge and effectuality. Going round the Pa Kua in a clockwise direction, we come to the east, Segment Three, which connects with family. Segment Four appears in the south-east, and means wealth. Directly south lies Segment Nine, signifying fame and reputation. South-west houses Segment Two, relationships and marriage. Segment Seven lies in the west and

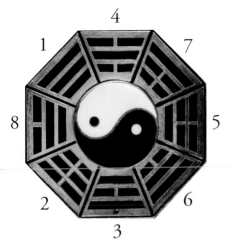

The Pa Kua is a powerful charm that works to restore harmony.

rearranging the relevant segment. Change will soon follow in your life. However, Feng Shui practitioners vary in the way they employ the Pa Kua – so Segment One, rather than being aligned with north, may be placed to coincide with the front door, meaning that as you enter your house you come into Segment One, your success area. Your wealth corner is then to your far left, your relationships corner to your far right, and so on. A mini-version of this can also be applied to a room, or even a desk. I have found this system to work very well.

relates to offspring. Coming full circle to the north-west and Segment Six, we arrive in the area of friends and helpful people. In the centre is Segment Five, the *Tai Chi*, or Supreme Potential. However, it must be said that the meanings of the segments vary according to different sources.

If you place the Pa Kua over a diagram of your house, you will be able to see what goes where. For instance, you will be able to locate your 'marriage' segment. If things are not going well in your relationships, you might like to examine that area. Is it cluttered and messy, or sparse and empty? You can immediately alter the Feng Shui by

It is easy to see how the nine squares or segments align with numerology. Practical Four connects with wealth, and high-minded Nine with fame; effectual Eight goes with knowledge, and harmony-loving Six aligns with friends. Perhaps less obvious is the connection of Seven with offspring, but with Seven we make magical changes in the world and there is nothing more magical than a child. 'Offspring' may also relate to the original things we create, using our ingenuity and imagination. Joyful Three relates to family, and this may be extended to include all the people and things that make life sparkle. In the centre we have Five, number of connection and communication – Segment Five touches each of the other squares, and in the Chinese system is

connected with balance, being the middle number between 1 and 9.

Once you have the general idea of Feng Shui, you can begin to experiment. It is very important not to make major changes or to expect swift results as it may take several weeks or months for a shift to take place. It is also important to remember the rule 'If it ain't broke, don't fix it' with Feng Shui. It may be tempting to rearrange every area of your life and in so doing cause upheaval – Feng Shui should be carefully targeted.

You can use Feng Shui to help balance your personality. For instance, if you lack Four and practicalities trip you up, tidy up your far left corner, ie Segment Four, your wealth area. Place a few coins there and/or a money plant. If Two is lacking and your relationships don't thrive, clear up your Segment Two in the far right, and place pairs of objects there, such as two doves, two teddy bears, or whatever appeals. If One is lacking and you don't seem to have much drive, make sure your entrance is clear in Segment One and that as you come in your front door you have a feeling of smooth movement, successful entry. If you want children or yearn to

Feng shui is a practical system, using spiritual forces to improve the environment.

explore life's mysteries and create transformation, place an ear of wheat in Segment Seven, in the right of your dwelling. Family and joy can be boosted by a lamp in Segment Three on the left, knowledge and power may be enhanced by books and trophies in the near left-hand Segment Eight, while Segment Nine, straight ahead, could be a good place for a symbol of success, such as the Sun. Place presents from friends in Segment Six, on your right as you come in. Segment Five, in the centre, might be a good place for your computer.

Any number that you need can be brought into your life with Feng Shui. You can play with ideas and make minor changes, to see how they work. If you cannot think of anything appropriate, placing a crystal in a segment is usually a good way to enhance it. Stand at your

doorway and imagine you are the life force or chi – where would you flow freely? Where might you get stuck, or rush too fast? You can adjust this, and it is especially important to do this if problems look likely to occur in areas corresponding to a number you lack. Lamps, wind-chimes, plants and ornaments can all be used. Of course, most homes are not square, and there may even be segments that seem missing – for instance if your dwelling is an L-shape. Invoke the energies of the missing section by placing appropriate artefacts close to where it should be – this is especially important if you are lacking the energies of the corresponding number.

Look also at your personal cycles (see pages 318–55) and attune to your current Personal Cycle Number. For instance, if you are going through a One year, to make the best of things it may be especially important that your Segment One, or entrance point, is clear and convenient. If you are in a Two cycle, it will be especially important to tend to your relationship corner, and so forth. Practical considerations obviously restrict your choices about what goes where, but with a bit of inventiveness you can change the energies of any space and bring some numerological principles into your life in a dynamic fashion with Feng Shui.

Numerology and Tarot

Reading Tarot cards is an ancient system of divination and many people believe it can provide the seeker with keys to deep insight. Tarot has many numerological links. The cards in the Tarot are grouped into the *Major Arcana* and the *Minor Arcana*.

The Major Arcana form a suit of 22 symbols that represent the bigger issues in life; 22 is a Master Number, which gives the foundation for collective goals. Each of the Major Arcana cards is numbered as follows:

0 The Fool
Unlimited possibilities and potential that may be taken for granted, or misused.

2 The High Priestess
Wisdom and intuition – emotions may mislead you.

1 The Magician
Will, initiative, creative thinking – nothing is 100% certain.

3 The Empress
Joy and fulfilment.

4 The Emperor

Wisdom through experience, the need to live life in the present and overcome fears.

7 The Chariot

Lessons from the forces of Nature deepening consciousness.

5 The Heirophant

Being able to appreciate the wide variety of experience in life.

8 Strength

Opposition uses up huge amounts of energy; going with the flow brings power.

6 The Lovers

Love, closeness, choice.

9 Hermit

Being alone is productive, but humour and interaction enable you to lift others, and be lifted.

10/1
Wheel of Fortune
Rebirth, and a possible new start.

13/4 Death
The reality of life involves death, but this card means transformation – change is the only constant.

11/2 Justice
Weighing up what is right for yourself and others.

14/5
Temperance
Let go of self-imposed limits and learn the lessons of life that lead to balance.

12/3
Hanged Man
Hesitation and resistance are a prelude to moving forwards, hopefully towards greater fulfilment.

15/6 Devil
Materialism and glamour can enslave you. Fears are of your own making.

16/7
The Tower
Upheaval, profound change, leading to revelation of inner truth.

19/1
The Sun
Vitality, success, achievement, mastery.

17/8
The Star
Spiritual blessings, fulfilment of goals, hope, wonder, inner power.

20/2
Judgement
The value of self-awareness, mindfulness, fairness, balance, detachment.

18/9
The Moon
Possible illusion, the subtle, the invisible, soul, imagination.

21/3
The World
Achievement, a task well completed, greater vision, potential.

The Minor Arcana form a suit of 56 cards, which reduces to 11/2, relating to uplifting and the potential for balance. The numbers 11 and 22 are both Master Numbers, inviting you to look at the wider picture. The Minor Arcana are composed of four suits: Wands, Pentacles, Swords and Cups, relating to Fire, Earth, Air and Water, respectively. Four relates to the building blocks of existence, and the

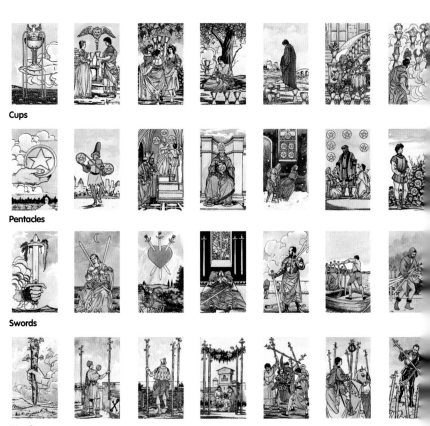

Cups

Pentacles

Swords

Wands

'Four' theme repeats in the fact that each of the suits has four 'court cards' – King, Queen, Knight and Page.

The colourful cards in the Tarot reflect archetypal themes.

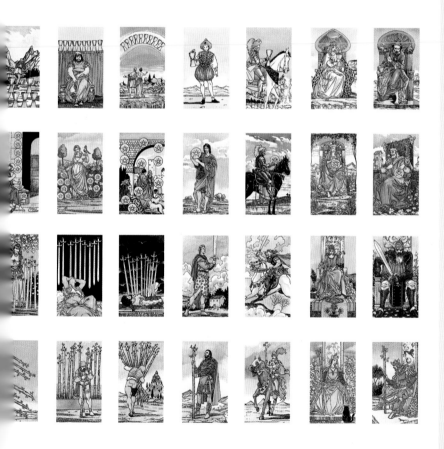

Numerology and the Qabalah

The Qabalah is a body of Hebrew mystical doctrine that has been used by many well-known occultists in the West – for instance Eliphas Levi, Aleister Crowley and MacGregor Mathers. The Qabalah is profound and subtle, requiring many years of deep study to comprehend, and its true meanings cannot be written down but only understood by initiation and experience.

Central to the Qabalah is the *Ets Chayyim*, or Tree of Life. The Tree of Life is also the body of the Cosmic Man, Adam Kadmon, and is represented by the Jewish *menorah*, or seven-branched candlestick. In effect it is a 'diagram of manifestation' starting with purest spirit and arriving at densest matter. On the journey from spirit to matter there are different 'categories of being', and these are represented by 10 spheres or *Sephiroth* (singular *Sephirah*). The Sephiroth are considered to have manifested in a fixed order, represented by the Path of the Lightning Flash, which determines the number assigned to each. Each of the Sephiroth has correspondences, or magical connections, that can be used in ritual, and the Sephiroth are connected by pathways that are explored through visualizations.

There are 22 pathways linking the Sephiroth. These correspond with the cards of the Major Arcana of the Tarot (see pages 86–9). The meanings of the cards reflect the types of experience to be encountered by the explorer and the wisdom that can be acquired. The small cards also link with the Tree – for instance, all Aces belong with Kether, all Twos with Chokmah, and so on. In addition, all Knights link with Chokmah, all Queens with Binah, all Kings with Tiphareth, and all Pages with Malkuth.

You can see that the characteristics of the numbers (see pages 20–59) don't link well with the numbers of the Sephiroth. Two, for instance, is the number of relationship and the Eternal Feminine, which sits uneasily with the image of Supernal Father. The sequence compares better when we regard Kether as the Great Zero, the infinity of potential; Chokmah then becomes One, the Initiator; Binah Two, the potential for Generation; Chesed Three, creativity and inspiration; Geburah Four, strength; Tiphareth Five, possibilities and discoveries; Netzach Six, art and community; Hod Seven, knowledge and hidden structure; Yesod Eight, power and organization moving with patterns and destiny; Malkuth Nine, fruitful culmination. However, there are still big problems with these associations – Four does not correlate with the breaking-down aspect of Geburah, despite some old associations of Four with negativity and misfortune. Nine, as one of the least materialistic numbers, is questionable as Malkuth, and so on.

Another correlation may be to use Malkuth as One, the starting point, Yesod Two, reflection and intuition, Hod Three, the creative potential of knowledge, Netzach Four, the sensuous fruits of practical gifts, Tiphareth Five, many potentials. The path could then be taken to Chesed, and the harmony and idealism of Six, moving across to Geburah which could be seen as deconstructing with the probing analysis of Seven. Binah then takes on the mantle of Eight – the power of pragmatism and the hand of destiny, and Chokmah becomes Nine, the culminator and dispenser of knowledge. Other links could also be made if you want to play with ideas.

These associations are by no means classical interpretations and would no doubt be regarded as sacrilege by Qabalists. The Qabalah is a matter for deep study and one of the lessons here is that the true essence of all things is to be explored with openness and a sense of wide possibilities. As you look into the numbers at an energy level, you move away from topics such as relationships and careers into much more subtle realms. A true exploration of the Qabalah may be the work of a lifetime.

The Qabalah has long been used in magic and inward exploration.

The Sephiroth

Each Sephirah has a number, which is considered significant, as follows:

1 Kether

The Crown. Purest existence. The Cosmos.

2 Chokmah

Wisdom. The Supernal Father. Energy without form – the great impregnator. The zodiac.

3 Binah

Understanding. The Supernal Mother. The roots of form. Saturn.

4 Chesed

Mercy. The Preserver. Organization and inspiration. Jupiter.

5 Geburah

Strength and Severity. Force, katabolism, necessary destruction. Mars.

6 Tiphareth

Beauty. The individuality. The Sun.

7 Netzach

Victory. Intuition, arts, dance, emotions. Venus.

8 Hod

Glory. Intellect, logical working. Mercury.

9 Yesod

Foundation. Images, the machinery of the Universe. The Moon.

10 Malkuth

Kingdom. Physical manifestation. The Earth.

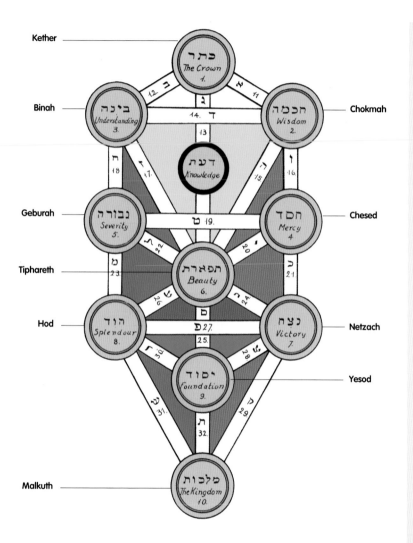

Kether

Binah

Chokmah

Geburah

Chesed

Tiphareth

Hod

Netzach

Yesod

Malkuth

3: Five Formulas

We are all made up of combinations of number 'vibrations' which are uncovered through the calculations of the various formulas discussed in this chapter. These include your Personality Number, Life Path Number, Soul Number, Destiny Number and Here-and-Now number.

Introduction to the Formulas

Numbers are all around us, in our lives and our actions. Some of them are obvious and some are more hidden. Some numbers are more important than others because we have them with us all the time. These influence our character and our destiny, through their special vibration. Recognizing these numbers can help us to become self-aware, to manage our lives and make the best of all our resources.

There are five main numbers that we carry with us throughout life. Some of these are unchanging; others may alter, either because we plan it that way or because it just happens. They are our:

- Personality Number
- Life Path Number
- Soul Number
- Destiny Number
- Here-and-Now Number

These may have different names given to them by different numerologists, but they add up to the same influence.

Always, when working out one of your numbers, keep adding the digits involved until they round down to a single-digit number, or 11 or 22, the Master Numbers (see pages 60–67), which carry both the quality of the single-digit number they add up to (respectively 2 and 4) and an extra

'something' which may be expressed, sometimes with extra effort.

Your Personality Number

This is derived from the day of the month that your birthday falls on.

Numbers 1–9 speak for themselves.

For higher numbers, add the digits together – for instance, if you were born on the 10th, then:

$$10=1+0=1.$$

So One is your Personality Number.

As another example, for the 28th:

$$28=2+8=10, 1+0=1.$$

So 28 also becomes One.

Your Personality Number will never change. You carry it with you through life and it is a very obvious number which appears on many documents. This number is an expression of your outward personality, the way you meet the world and the impression you make. Although it goes deep, permeating through all your experience and all you do, it is also on the surface. It makes a statement about you. Often a person's Personality Number will be one of the most obvious things you notice when you first get to know them.

Your Life Path Number

This is found by totalling all the digits in your birthdate.

For instance, if you were born on 26th October 1972 you would write it as:

$$2+6+1+0+1+9+7+2=28, 2+8=10, 1+0=1.$$

So your Life Path Number is One.

The Life Path Number is also something unchangeable. It relates to the path you are on, your tasks and self-development. As you get to know someone a little better, the direction they are taking, or choosing, becomes more evident.

The Life Path number is unchangeable, and in some ways is linked to spirit.

Your Soul Number

This is arrived at by adding the value of the vowels in your name, for these are the out-breath of your essence.

In the case of Jane Mary Jones, we have:

A+E+A+Y+O+E

1+5+1+7+6+5=25, 2+5=7

So she has a Soul Number of Seven.

Note that Y is sometimes a vowel and sometimes a consonant: the Y in 'Mary' is considered a vowel, but the Y in 'yellow' is considered a consonant. W can also be counted as a vowel in some locations; the Welsh 'cwm' is an example.

Your Soul Number tells of your instincts and feelings, and may also be about the groups you connect with on a cultural and intuitive level. This number may not be so conscious at first, and people who get to know you may gradually become aware of this deeper self and its values – in fact they may be more aware of it than you are, so natural may it be to you. Your Soul Number may be about your yearnings and dreams, even your purpose in living.

This is found by translating each of the letters in your full name (as it appears on your birth certificate) into numbers.

The letters go from 1 to 9 and then start at 1 again:

1	2	3	4	5	6	7	8	9
A	B	C	D	E	F	G	H	I
J	K	L	M	N	O	P	Q	R
S	T	U	V	W	X	Y	Z	

(In the ancient Hebrew alphabet letters also served as numbers, and some numerologists approximate the old Hebrew letters into the modern letters. This system is not so straightforward – see page 13. You may use this system if you like, but we are creatures of the 21st century, and, while our alphabet may not have the same esoteric links, it is what we work with in our lives.) Here is an example:

J A N E   M A R Y   J O N E S

1+1+5+5+4+1+9+7+1+6+5+5+1=51, 5+1=6

Her Destiny Number is Six.

This number relates to family heritage, to the expectations that are placed upon you, and the ones you have for yourself. It reflects the path you are on in life in a more subtle way and is less about what you create and more about what you learn. You may change your name through choice or marriage, and this will have an effect on your destiny, which will overlay the original number, and may become more important. However, the original Destiny Number stays with you. If you change your name, consider all relevant numbers.

Your Here-and-Now Number

This number comes from your Christian name, nickname and/or the name you are generally known by, among friends, family and colleagues. It holds a very important 'vibration' because you may hear it many times a day. You may have more than one Here-and-Now Number in different situations.

This number is very powerful and very obvious, but not so deep. It reveals the way you are seen on an immediate level and also the image you wish to project. It is like a strong wave passing through the surface of your life, but it may leave the depths undisturbed. This number is the easiest to change, and if you want to shift your numerology profile you could start with a new nickname in a new group of friends and see what happens.

Your numerology profile

When you have worked out all your numbers, you can see how you are made up and then you may get some idea of the potential conflicts and complements within you. We are all complex creatures, and, while you may have more impact if you have several numbers the same, your experience may be richer with a variety of numbers. Never see yourself as a passive victim of your numbers – you can make the best of what you are given, and there are hints for doing this in each of the following chapters.

Your numerological profile begins at birth, and continues with your naming.

1 as Your Personality Number

Wherever you are, wherever you go, you need to make an impact. Maybe you like to dress in some noticeable way, speak and talk loudly or tell other people what to do. One thing is for certain, no one is going to boss you around and if they try they will regret it. If you have gentler numbers like Two or Six also strong in your make-up, you may sometimes feel uncomfortable at the way you come across, but who cares? The worst thing would be to feel repressed, ignored or put down.

Although you are always zooming around, making things happen, you are not necessarily a leader – you don't want the trouble of organizing other people.

Tips

- At the end of each day, always count what you *have* done, to get that sense of achievement
- Get small achievements under your belt first, so you feel you are moving ahead – this will hearten you for the longer tasks
- Try something new regularly, each day or each week
- Don't try to be different – your natural individuality shines through better when you are relaxed

While you love a bit of applause, you are happiest doing your own thing. Having to consider other people cramps your style and can even make you feel panicky and confused. You want to feel you have made a meaningful contribution and that you have helped some person or cause, but then you move on to the next challenge. You can be a bit of an achievement junkie, always looking for your next 'fix', which is something created, something vanquished, and so on.

People will see you as the supreme individualist, and you come across as confident and determined. You may not always feel it, however, and if attacked you may feel hollow and wobbly. To compensate for this, you may act

Expressing your One personality can get you noticed and respected.

arrogantly and even a bit aggressively. Try to avoid this – it will dissipate your energies and make you feel dissatisfied in more ways than one.

You have a strong sense of your own individuality and you are focused and determined. You really *hate* to be slowed down, and the 'small print' drives you crazy. It is important to realize that time devoted to sorting out hitches and details is time well spent and, even if there is nothing concrete or impressive to show for it, the hours you put in are all part of the process of getting somewhere – which you will undoubtedly do in the end.

One personalities often try very hard, competing with themselves.

1 as Your Life Path Number

You are probably quite aware that you stand or fall by your own efforts. This is not necessarily because you have no one to help you, or even that you don't trust anyone. It is just that you know, deep down, that you are not going to be the person you want and need to be if you don't do it yourself. This does not mean that you do *everything* yourself. There will be tasks and activities that are outside your range of skills, and you are only too happy to hand these over.

You can be incredibly single-minded and focused, which means you achieve impressive things that may leave others gasping. With One as your Life Path Number, you are sure to succeed substantially. However, you may have blind spots. There are certain things you may forget about completely, which rise up at some inconvenient time to trouble you. At other times, a certain naïvety can trip you up. You assume that others will carry out the tasks they have been given in the same dedicated way that you do – it can be a shock to find that someone just has not delivered. Then for a while you may be completely thrown, as things collapse around you. Every so often your life may fall apart, or seem to – but like a phoenix you always rise up from the ashes and soar towards the sky, leaving a trail of sparks in your wake.

To do

- Make a list of what you want to complete each day, and carry forward anything that does not get done until the next day
- Consciously set high aims and review your progress
- Make a note of your mistakes – they are fantastic learning opportunities

Famous people

- George Washington 22.2.1732
- Florence Nightingale 12.5.1820
- George Clooney 6.5.1961
- Tiger Woods 30.12.1975

It is important that you choose a path in life that enables you to make your mark in a unique way. Be courageous. It may be better to be a big fish in a small pond than to lose your self-image in a large lake full of other big fish. You must always have a result to aim for. Ignore anyone who tells you to relax – you cannot let it all hang out unless you have a sense of achievement. However, you do need to ensure that you are not too driven, and one way to achieve this is to set 'balance and adequate rest' as one of your goals.

With One as your Life Path you will only feel 'right' if you make your mark.

1 as Your Soul Number

Your inner self whispers to you of solitude and self-sufficiency, and you may secretly long for times when you can be on your own. You may even feel a bit ashamed of this, partly because it is very hard to communicate these feelings to anyone else. In the end you need to accept that others will find it hard to understand you, and there is no reason why they should. Once you realize that all that matters is that you meet your own standards and feel comfortable with yourself, you experience the true freedom you yearn for.

However, being on your own does not mean going off into a dream, or meditating – it means having the opportunity to take action, totally untrammelled by anybody's influence or expectations. Peace may not be your priority – you can feel independent in a crowd as long as they leave you alone.

You seek 'the road less travelled' and feel fulfilled if others follow you – not because you need their company but because it means you have blazed a meaningful trail. You yearn to create something totally new and you will only find peace if you make a unique contribution, however small, though you have grand ambitions.

Mantras and images

- My way or the highway
- I shine like the sun at midday
- I can and do look after myself
- My creativity flows in a constant stream
- There are no limits to my big ideas
- Life is simple
- The journey of a thousand miles starts with the first step

The simplicity of nature is hugely inspiring to the One soul.

The urge to individuality is very powerful inside you and it needs to find positive expression, or you could find that you unconsciously sabotage things for yourself and others. You may get very irritable if you are disturbed. You could insist on doing something alone that really does need two or more for safety or efficiency. Ask yourself what you are trying to prove. If this happens, you are wasting time and energy that could go towards bringing you the satisfaction of real creativity. Emotionally you are quite self-sufficient and, while you can be demanding in relationships, control means more to you than closeness. In fact you may not need love quite as much as some other people and that is nothing to be ashamed of. You are always fair, loyal and reliable.

111

1 as Your Destiny Number

You have the gift of vision – not necessarily in a psychic sense, but in your ability to visualize future goals and see the way to achieving them. Others sense this and often look towards you as a leader. You may assume that role, and indeed you are generally comfortable with it. However, you don't really like to have to organize other people, and sometimes it may seem as if their expectations are a heavy burden to carry. Taking the lead may seem like the lesser of two evils, because one thing you definitely don't want to do is follow someone else.

In your family you were, and are, probably regarded as unique or exceptional in some way. When small you may have been singled out as having some special talent, and a great deal may have been expected of you. It could feel as if it is up to you to redeem your family in some form or fashion, or at least show a good example to the world. You may have been given responsibility and independence at a young age. You may have always felt alone, however much support you were given, and possibly misunderstood.

It is possible for you to go one of two ways. You may well rebel and strike off on your own path, determined not to conform to anyone else's wishes. On the other hand, you may go the way that is expected of you, intent on being the brightest, the best and the first. Stop and reflect on what is right for you – to rebel for the sake of it could be counter-productive; to follow a pre-set course could be frustrating. It is better to use your far-sightedness to steer a course that will bring deep fulfilment, and prove you *really* don't care what anyone says or thinks.

Lessons to learn

- Being truly unique means measuring yourself by one standard alone – your own
- Incorporate others into your vision and be patient – arguments will hold you up
- If what you have started is worth doing, then finish it

As a One your strength may have been spotted at an early age.

1 as Your Here-and-Now Number

Sometimes you wonder why you are the person who is always singled out. The meal is poor, so who is the one to speak to the restaurant manager? A kitten is stuck up a tree, so who climbs after it? Whenever there is an unfamiliar or scary situation, your friends seem to expect you to lead them out of trouble or into something entertaining. Most of the time you oblige brilliantly, but often you would rather not.

Make it work for you

- There is no need to take yourself too seriously – people will be impressed if you laugh at yourself
- Make an effort to listen to others – then you won't miss something that is key
- Concentrate on short-term, focused goals, so that you excel with minimal effort
- Play to your strengths – things can be easier than you assume

You love to stand out from your crowd and quite often do your best to be just that little bit different. You are a bit like an 'A-list' celebrity, and if you have got it you flaunt it. You are competitive – you don't have to be the best at everything, but there must be one or two things you do better than anyone else, and if you cannot excel you would rather not bother at all. At such times, you may find an excuse to go off on your own, and you may get quite upset.

Although you may have more than your fair share of the limelight, you probably don't have many close friends. Anyone who is a true friend is very valuable to you, for it means they are prepared to accept your rather tough and pushy exterior and see the real you underneath. Depending on the other numbers in your make-up, you may not be nearly as confident as you seem. One as a Here-and-Now Number can be quite difficult, as it may isolate you when that is not what you want at all. However, when you are around, people sit up and take notice, there is usually something interesting afoot, and things move forward.

With a One Here-and-Now number you can never be just a face in the crowd.

2 as Your Personality Number

Who is always putting people at their ease, bustling about in the back room making sure everything is organized for comfort and efficiency? Probably it is a Number Two, whose mission in life is to spread a little happiness or, failing that, at least contentment. If a disagreement develops between your friends, you are the one who breaks it up and skilfully manages to get each person to appreciate the other's point of view.

If you are really on top form, your intuition may warn you of trouble on the horizon and you may be able to stop the arguments in their tracks by changing the subject or creating a diversion. Although you detest aggression, you quite like situations where your peacemaking prowess is called for – in fact being needed is what matters most to you, and occasionally you may verge on the sycophantic in your efforts to please.

You may well be known in your circle for your fabulous 'tea and sympathy'. When friends' lives fall apart, yours is the shoulder they cry on. You may find all too often that you are the one who gets the phone call in the middle of the night, but you don't always get the thanks you deserve because it can be easy for people to take you for granted. Your capacity for accepting the foibles of your friends seems endless, but then suddenly, to the surprise of everyone, you may take umbrage at something comparatively small and then it is you that has to be calmed down.

You are at your best when you listen to your instincts. If you have to use logic to make a decision, you procrastinate endlessly, and in the end may stubbornly pursue a course that is totally irrational, to the consternation of all who care about you. Try not to get to this point.

If you find yourself driven mad by the effort of trying to evaluate the pros and cons, go off and listen to some soothing music, until you feel calm enough to hear the voice within. Sometimes you can feel so buffeted by the views and demands of others that your own wishes are lost without trace – don't let that happen. Your calm and charming self is too valuable for that.

Companions are valuable, but never be afraid to follow your own direction.

Tips

- Avoid being placed on the spot – 'get-out' clauses should be your speciality
- When your fears overtake you, remember it is often better to regret what you *have* done, rather than what you *haven't* done
- Feel the fear and do it anyway – it cannot be that bad
- Keep a compliments diary to raise your spirits when you imagine people are treating you with contempt
- Ask for support – people cannot read your mind

2 as Your Life Path Number

As you walk through life, you need a partner in all you do. This can be a great thing or a recipe for heartache and frustration – it all depends on how good you are at choosing. Try not to be so needy that you gravitate towards the first person who seems to want you. This applies not only to loving relationships but also to friendships and business connections. In a couple, you will achieve much more than you would alone, and you have the art of sharing and compromise down to a fine degree.

You don't need to hog the limelight and will often feel genuinely content to be the power behind the throne. But in the end this all has to add up to something meaningful. The danger is that you could be used, and become subsumed within a more demanding personality, or even drawn into dubious dealings – this can happen if you lose sight of reality and think the *relationship* is everything when truly the point is not to be gazing at each other but moving in tandem towards a shared goal.

So what sort of 'shared goal' might fulfil you? Something that generates love and compassion outside the narrow orbit of personal concerns. Something that involves balance, peace and harmony. The theme of self-awareness, and true perception, runs throughout. Even though you may feel strongly about diplomacy

To do

- If you feel hurt, talk about this to a trusted friend – another perspective always helps
- Take time out to meditate and get in touch with your intuition
- Always have something to nurture

and tolerance, occasionally you can be pitched into taking sides. Once forced to enter the fray, you may see yourself as in a position where you can only win or lose, and you may fight blindly, and therefore jeopardizing your achievements and peace of mind. There is no need for this – your challenge is always to see the connections and to raise things to a

Being together but not 'joined at the hip' is the key to fulfilment.

Famous people

- Gustav Mahler 7.7.1860
- Isadora Duncan 27.5.1878
- Keith Richards 18.12.1943
- Coco Chanel 19.8.1883

level where conflicts are not so much resolved as irrelevant.

It is crucial for you to have the correct support in whatever you do, so ensure this is in place. Your first responsibility must always be to yourself, so protect your vulnerabilities. Only from a position of strength will you be able to help others.

2 as Your Soul Number

Most people dream of a soulmate, but for you this could amount to a preoccupation, as you believe you just cannot be complete unless you have that person in your life. Needless to say, this can cause you a great deal of heartache if it does not go right. Sadly, 'going right' may not be easy, because you may be quite a perfectionist and even critical of potential partners, and so you may feel life has let you down when what you need is a bigger dose of compromise.

If you do meet someone, it may be hard for you to give them the space that everyone – and every relationship – needs, as you try to live joined at the hip. The truth is that soulmates are often brought together to teach each other something rather than to walk hand-in-hand into the sunset. When you are ready, you will meet your 'twin flame' – a much more meaningful relationship where you can truly accomplish something as a couple rather than disappear inside yourselves. You are on a search for wisdom, and tranquillity.

Sharing something makes the world radiant to your Two soul.

Mantras and images

- I do not judge my brother until I have walked a mile in his moccasins
- Tea for two and two for tea, me for you and you for me
- Love walks with me so I am never alone
- Two heads are better than one
- I am balanced and in harmony
- A quiet life and a peaceful one

If you allow yourself to relax and trust in the love that is all around you, you may find almost as much fulfilment in the natural world as you might in human company. Nature can provide you with an inspiring counterpoint, showing you deep truths on an instinctual level. Don't let the prevailing patterns of our culture throw you. Some of the things you learn cannot be put into words and you don't have to

try – you will find a way to live that warms your heart even if you cannot find the words for it. Life is simple, but you may muddy the waters by becoming over-emotional and in effect almost looking for situations where you have an axe to grind. This may be because you feel something is missing – if so, true wisdom comes when you realize you have had it inside you all along.

2 as Your Destiny Number

As you were growing up, it is probable that fairness was an issue in some way. This may have been because you were expected to look after a sibling and/or responsible for harmony in the home, because there was a conspicuous effort to be fair (which, in some strange way, can create a situation where everyone is always comparing their portions), or because the situation was obviously very *unfair*, and this would understandably be an issue for you.

You can learn to rise above this and to see that fairness is not a matter of hair-splitting or pounds of flesh, but rather about an atmosphere of consideration and respect. At your best you can foster this.

Others may look to you to make decisions for them and you may excel at this. You are great at identifying the issues and weighing everything up. When it comes to your own concerns, however, things may not be so clear; while you may force yourself to make decisions, you may then agonize over whether you have done the right thing, and berate yourself about any mistakes you make. Your standards in general are quite high and you are something of a perfectionist.

Your task is to learn the art of compromise. This does not mean compromising with others – you are probably expert at that and at keeping all of the people happy all of the time. The important thing is to find a comfortable compromise between the ideal and the achievable. There is no need

to be discontented and dissatisfied with yourself because you are less than perfect. Learn to see the beauty in yourself, for like all of creation you are flawed, and it is those flaws that make you special, sending you on a quest for what may make you complete. That 'quest' is the essence of what makes a relationship. With this in mind, you can make deeply satisfying relationships with other people and with your environment.

Lessons to learn

- Accept your own feelings and needs, for these are part of the equation
- Accept disharmony sometimes – in the end it can lead to a deeper understanding
- 'Beauty is truth, truth beauty' – remember this

Sometimes not taking things too seriously can help relationships and make plans fall into place.

2 as Your Here-and-Now Number

Playing matchmaker, soothing hurt feelings, making sure there is a place for everything and everything is in its place – what would they all do without you? No one is indispensable, but you would be missed more than most even if you don't get the appreciation you deserve. However, you are not interested in applause – a 'thank you' is always nice, but you get a buzz out of seeing things go smoothly and smiles on faces.

You can be quite shy – the idea of taking a bow makes you blush all over. Actually you may be a bit afraid that if you get noticed too much you will be judged.

Make it work for you

- Get a friend to help you out with boring tasks – having a giggle together will work wonders
- If you do something good, make sure folks know it was you – this does not have to put you in the spotlight but can avoid the unfairness of being upstaged
- If you start worrying, ask yourself if it will matter next year – if not, forget it
- Plan a secret treat for yourself

Being 'weighed and found wanting' is a fear of yours, so you try to do your best all the time.

Depending on what other numbers there are in your chart, you may sometimes feel really fed up with catering to others' whims, and this can make you snappy and spiteful. You may find yourself whispering nasty gossip to your best friend. It is not that you want to be cruel or that you get a kick out of contemplating other people's difficulties and disgraces; it is just that you spend a lot of time keeping your own emotions in check and your needs in the background, so the negativity has to come out somewhere.

It will help if you realize that being ambivalent is not a crime and that a little hypocrisy and 'two-facedness' are natural to most people. Of course you don't want to let this side of you run amok – just

being self-aware, self-forgiving and a little self-indulgent at times will help. You can enjoy appearing perfect without really being so, and, before you start worrying about being found out, rest assured that most people are far too concerned with themselves to be that observant.

Doing things together gives you motivation and makes you feel appreciated.

3 as Your Personality Number

In the middle of a laughing crowd or on a pleasure trip, there is usually something happening around you, and if not there soon will be, if you have any say in the matter. It is your mission to put a smile on every face, and this makes you top of most guest lists. You may appear to be the party animal through and through, but sometimes you withdraw into your dreams, and occasionally you just get fed up with it all. At times like that you may find that you cannot be bothered, and you may even turn into a 'couch potato', waiting for something good just to turn up.

You can be a bit of a 'motormouth' and, while what comes out is usually witty and entertaining, occasionally you cannot resist the temptation to gossip or poke fun. If you do this, you are sacrificing long-term satisfaction for a short-term buzz. Yes, you may be raising a giggle, but what are people really thinking? Will they trust you as a friend? What feelings about you are lurking behind that grin? If you want your popularity to go deep, make sure you stay kind and charitable.

The world of the arts and entertainment is important to you. It could be a good idea to get involved in amateur dramatics or in

Tips

- Make the most of every opportunity – you cannot be sure it will still be there when you are in the mood to bother
- Don't listen to anyone who tells you to do one thing at a time – you need to flit from task to task
- Prioritize – it is fun to have lots going on, but what is going to lead to the most opportunities?
- Bite your tongue before saying anything negative about anyone

Even as adults we learn so much about life through play.

organizing team sports and outings. Often you leave the details to chance and with your luck you generally succeed, but not always. Try not to have too many projects going at once, and enlist some reliable help – you may have to share a bit of the limelight but you can out-sparkle the competition with little effort. Always leave yourself room to change your mind

because if something more appealing comes along you will be chasing it, and you could let people down. Generally you are a lucky person, and this may seem magical but actually it comes from your positive attitude. Take care that you don't lose this by fretting about things you have missed – concentrate on what brings you real fulfilment.

3 as Your Life Path Number

Expressing yourself and creating something that gives others pleasure is your primary drive. Enabling other people to communicate and move their lives onwards is a major motivator for you. You see yourself as making the world a better place – not through some over-arching ideology, but through shared schemes, games and imaginative enterprises. You need freedom and must be able to act spontaneously, because opportunity knocks here, there and everywhere and you are the servant of serendipity.

There is a great joy in living, but it is not enough for you merely to experience this – you want to inspire it. You may develop the gift of persuasive rhetoric so you can charm the birds out of the trees, but you also like to hear other people speaking their thoughts and ideas. You probably are a great 'brainstormer' – you are in your element where lots of crazy notions are sparking, and you feel something fabulous is just around the corner. It is, but you won't be contented with it. There will always be something brighter and better to aim for.

Sometimes you may feel that however much you say you are not really heard, or however much happiness you spread you have not quite done enough. You have a 'divine discontent' that can spur you on. Your name may be up in lights and the glittering prizes won, but there is always

something more to explore. Other people may think you are never satisfied, but you are mostly just enjoying the journey. You need to choose a path that will give

To do

- Express any talent you have (music, poetry, art, writing) – just because it comes easily does not mean it is not worth developing
- Play is a serious business – children learn through it and so do you, so make time for it
- Always have a project on the go – better to start something and change your mind than not to do anything

you flexibility and, while a few deadlines may concentrate you, you must always have the leisure to play. If things go sour, don't go into a 'to-hell-with-it-all' mood. You will need to go through some dark patches as your subconscious is readjusting to a fresh course, and when this happens you should take time out to relax, play sport and spend time with people you like, until fresh motivation takes you.

Famous people

- F Scott Fitzgerald 24.9.1896
- Joan Rivers 8.6.1933
- John Travolta 18.2.1954
- John Grisham 8.2.1955

You need apportunities to free that creative 'Three' spirit within.

3 as Your Soul Number

Your heart is often filled with joy – there seems to be so much in life that is wonderful, and you are happy wallowing in it. A great hedonist, you have a way of celebrating through experiencing pleasure. Happiness, humour, sensuality, gratification – these are all divine gifts. Although you may not put it into words or even recognize it, the way you throw yourself into them is an act of worship, so deep does it go with you.

Dwelling on the sad or the negative is not for you, and when others introduce gloomy or demanding topics you move swiftly on. People may sometimes mistake this for superficiality, but it is nothing of the sort. Never doubt those instincts that focus on the light and the bright. Be an entertainer and tell those jokes even if some fall on stony ground, because there is a silver lining to all things and you are the one to reveal it. People usually find you a tonic to be with. You love fashion, retail therapy and nightlife – a real 'cheer-me-up' person. But you are not a great one for soggy heart-to-hearts – you would rather stow the tissues and crack open the bubbly.

You have one of the greatest gifts – that of living in the 'precious present'. Yesterday has gone and tomorrow never comes. Now there are flowers to pluck, animals to pet and children to have fun with – a child at heart yourself, you may lose yourself in

Mantras and images

- Happiness is a choice rather than a gift
- What I love is all around in earth and sky
- Laughter is a medicine that heals all ills
- Where is the party?
- When the going gets tough, the tough go shopping
- My whole body is smiling

playing games. You can be adept at getting on the same level as a child and therefore you may bring out the best in them as you genuinely enter into their interests – giggling, skipping about, smeared with mud or paint, but always stylish. You long for a playmate to enjoy life with, but your light heart can be taken for 'light weight', leaving you unfulfilled and wistful. Keep trusting to luck, for what you want will find you. Continue trying to express yourself, because this is vital to you, but think laterally as music and poetry may work where normal words fail.

3 as Your Destiny Number

So much to do, so little time. Sometimes it seems your brain is overflowing with all the possibilities you perceive and conceive. It may also feel as if you are surrounded by long faces, waiting for you to cheer them up. When you were a child, it may have been your task to act the clown and make everybody laugh; while you were no doubt good at this, at times you may have felt dispirited because there was not much fun in it for you.

Possibly you were regarded as the lucky one, and people may have been jealous of you. But you also may have felt the nip of the 'green-eyed monster', as you feared some people were more gifted and talented, and might steal the limelight.

You have some special talent or ability, and you need to find this and extend it. You probably have been regarded as 'talented' by others, but the qualities they have spotted and encouraged may not be the ones that will truly fulfil you. You love to be popular and it goes against the grain to provoke disapproval, but you may have to do this, at least temporarily, if you are to realize your true potential. It is up to you to sell yourself and the things that you are good at, or at least develop a genuine attitude of 'I couldn't care less'. Certain people may regard you as a child – you don't have anything to prove. The 'child self' has its own instinctual wisdom, and if

you have the courage to follow its whims you will be rewarded. There are things you know deep down that you can communicate through creativity. This may be through art, music or something you do with your hands. What you create does not have to be durable – like sand-paintings it may be washed away. Yet, if you touch lives, it has been worthwhile.

Lessons to learn

- The only applause worth hearing will come from people who truly understand your purpose, and from your own heart
- Words have a power that is almost magical – use them well
- Don't waste energy or pretend not to care when you do

You have so much to give through any art form without being perfect.

3 as Your Here-and-Now Number

Superficial? So what. If you could help the starving millions you would, but since you cannot do that you would much rather think about what you are doing on Saturday night and which new pair of shoes you will wear, to show yourself off. Your ambition is to be dressed in the latest gear, turning every head as you move on the dance floor, or to impress all your friends by playing in a band, or to have your own art exhibition in the local gallery, or preferably all three – and more.

Really you would like to be famous, but you don't mind what for. There are lots of things you could do, but you probably get too bored to stick at anything for very long, and you are perfectly happy flitting from one interest to another.

You have a wicked tongue and you are not too worried whose reputation you shred as long as everyone is amused – which they invariably are. If anyone gets upset, you reckon they should get over it – what is the point of being so sensitive? It is not that you are spiteful or vindictive; it is just that most things are not worth taking seriously. You will chat to anyone and bring them out of their shell – you are not judgemental and you can usually find

something in anyone to make you smile. It makes you feel really good when you get the awkward geek up on to the dance floor or raise a laugh from 'Ms Snooty' with a risqué joke. You are an incorrigible flirt, but you never mean to break anyone's heart – it is all for fun.

However, depending on the other numbers in your character, you may not always be comfortable with your frivolous image. You may even feel guilty about some of what you say and do, but when you try to make amends you find it hard not to slip into role and be flippant. Secretly you fear you are not that special and you may feel driven to keep proving it. Trust in your talents, and sparkle.

Whatever the occasion a smile costs nothing and gives everyone a lift.

Make it work for you

- Belief in yourself is the only thing that counts – talent is common, confidence is rare
- Never hesitate to say 'sorry' – you can charm your way into anyone's good books
- When you want to impress, keep it simple and easy
- There are plenty of easy ways to get in the local paper – study it and make your plan
- Have a go at talent shows, competitions, etc – you have to be in it to win it

Enjoy bringing colour and enthusiasm to everything you do.

4 as Your Personality Number

'Let's get down to basics' may be one of your favourite phrases, as you seek a firm foundation for everything, from your funds to your friendships. Patient and persevering, you like to do the organizing – you are the one who books the table, sorts out the transport and remembers the tickets. People know they can rely on you, and your circle of friends respect you for doing what you say you will do. Pity you cannot say the same for them. You often find other people unreliable, and your attitude is 'If you want a job done, do it yourself'.

Four can be a serious number when you find time to unwind.

Tips

- Take time out to enjoy physical pleasures such as massage and aromatherapy – these will keep you good-humoured
- Remember you are unique and that your 'finishative' is worth more than buckets of failed initiative
- Trust friends when they compliment you – believe you are giving something of value
- If you feel yourself getting depressed, *do something about it immediately* – don't let it get a hold

You can be mistrustful and pessimistic at times. It is very important for you to try to focus on all the good things you get from others, and to resolutely ignore the negative; otherwise it can grow out of proportion to the point where it can almost immobilize you. The converse to this is the fact that you notice all the small things, and can take great delight in acts of kindness, which you love to return.

You are unlikely to set the world alight and you have no intention of trying. Far too risky. Security is your goal, and you probably have modest but definite ideas of the standards you want to achieve – and achieve them you will, as sure as the sun rises each morning. A creature of habit, you can be found in the same place at the same time each day and folk can set their clocks by you. Boring? You cannot

see why. Surely the most important thing in life is to know where you are. Just below the surface of consciousness, your realism puts you in touch with the grim truths that some prefer to ignore. War, famine, disaster – these are realities to so many people on this earth and you know that survival depends on getting on with it. This you do with stunning efficiency. You are the one who sorts out the red tape and small print for 'airhead' friends and puts the kettle on when trouble strikes. If your take on things is a little gloomy, at least you have some practical help to offer. In order to make the best of life, you need to get properly in contact with your body, so that you can relax and enjoy tactile things. You also need to recognize that you are special. Anyone can giggle and make a spectacle, but you get things done and that is what counts.

4 as Your Life Path Number

If possible you will have your life mapped out, determined to proceed from birth to death in an orderly fashion. You set yourself milestones of achievement and may want to do things on schedule – go to university, get a job, get married, have kids, in the correct order and at the right time. To your credit, you mostly do what you set out to do. People may marvel at the way your life comes under control.

You are aware of your abilities and you trust your knowledge and experience, but sometimes your calm exterior is little more than skin deep, and you may be anxious about potential disasters. If things don't go to plan, however, you manage very well, adjusting your expectations and reverting to Plan B. In fact you cope with real trouble much better than you deal with the imaginary kind.

You will probably be happiest dealing with practical things – fantasy and emotion can be too distracting. If something is not useful, or will not enhance your creature comforts, or those of your loved ones or humanity at large, you cannot see the point. Your strength certainly does lie with the material and the functional, but don't let this blind you to the possibility that there may be other dimensions to life.

To do

- Put 'relax', 'go out for a meal', 'go to the cinema' and so on in your diary, and stick to those dates as rigidly as you do to work and duty commitments
- Do something with your hands, such as model-building, painting or pottery
- At the end of each day, write down three things that have brought you joy

Solid achievement brings a sense of achievement for Four.

Just because you cannot, or have not, experienced something does not mean it cannot exist. If you close your mind totally, you may end up with a sense of meaninglessness and even hopelessness. However, if you can just entertain the possibility that there may be more to existence than you imagine, you can lift your effectuality to something truly impressive.

Self-reliant and responsible, you may work endlessly to build something for yourself and your family, maybe forgoing holidays and weekends off. You derive satisfaction from this, but you also need to remember that all work and no play makes a person dull, and possibly unwell too. Apply your common sense to your own well-being, and not only will you get more done, but you will also find that you enjoy it.

Famous people

- Henri Matisse 31.12.1869
- Dolly Parton 19.1.1946
- Oprah Winfrey 29.1.1954
- Bill Gates 28.10.1955

4 as Your Soul Number

You long to be the rock that others can lean on, and however good you may be at this you often feel haunted by the times you may have inadvertently let someone down. Keeping people safe, secure and well cared-for is a deep drive within you. You realize that the body is a distillation of the spirit – in fact to you we all *are* our bodies, and you want to cherish and protect.

Sometimes you may set yourself impossible tasks, trying to preserve what is essentially ephemeral. If only forever really could be forever; if only some things really did last and remain unchanged. In the end you realize that what does endure is love, and each moment, if properly lived, is a kind of eternity. Living with the here-and-now and in contact with the evidence of your senses can bring you joy, and you are a deeply patient and gentle soul.

Tactile pursuits give you Four the feeling that all is well with the world.

The arts may appeal to you and you may lose yourself in the technical appreciation

Mantras and images

- I am a flower, beautiful and with deep roots
- Rome wasn't built in a day
- Gently does it
- It is hip to be square
- Comfort zone beats rolling stone
- Better safe than sorry
- I am steady as a rock
- Built for comfort, not speed

of paintings and ceramics. You are less interested in the symbolic and abstract – you admire a faithful representation of life. The earth and the countryside nourish you, and feeling your feet on solid ground gives you satisfaction. Growing things may fill you with wonder. Gardening may be an inspiration, for you may be able to appreciate the 'ordinary' magic of the sprouting seed rather than anything
more esoteric.

You yearn to be invincible – not necessarily so you can have power over others, but more to be able to cope with whatever life throws at you. It is important to you to test your strength and to build on it so you can deal with more and more, so you may set yourself tests of endurance. Others may realize you are doing this, when for you it is subconscious. They
may think you are purposely making life difficult, but they may not understand why. You are building emotional and mental (and possibly physical) muscle, and sooner or later you, and they, may be thankful for it.

The simple magic of nature can move you deeply.

4 as Your Destiny Number

You may feel that your life is quite strictly mapped out for you by your family and/or society at large, and that it is your task to discharge practical responsibilities. Possibly you will have to support others financially and physically. It may seem as if any desires and ambitions that you have are irrelevant and have to be suppressed or ignored – why should they count? It is up to you to do your duty, is it not?

As life goes by, you will probably build many things of enduring worth and there will probably be people who have a lot to thank you for. However, you may often feel that something is missing, and sometimes you may ask yourself why you are on this treadmill and whether this is really what you want. The truth of the matter is that you probably can derive deep satisfaction from your practical achievements and your possessions – money, car, house – but, because you may feel deprived of choices in life, resentment can spoil things. One day you will wake up to appreciate all you have done and to realize that you are where you want to be after all.

You have a wonderful ability to remain calm when everything around you is chaos, and to be a port in the storm for others. You keep a sense of perspective and are able to take things in bite-sized pieces, until you have sorted it all. However, secretly you long for someone to come along and take everything off your hands. You keep tabs on everything – from legal documents to DIY, you have it all at your fingertips. Yet in some small areas of your life you have little or no

Lessons to learn

- True liberty comes from getting satisfaction from doing what has to be done, and doing it gladly
- Identify what is truly your duty, not just what you have blindly accepted, or have thrust upon you by others
- Build for lasting benefit, but also teach others to do this for themselves

control, and may be quite childlike. For instance, your diet may be poor (you may 'comfort eat') or your driving may show pent-up frustration. It is important to allow yourself outlets for your feelings and to relinquish control of certain areas to someone else, so you can have playtime.

Once you realise that relaxing and having fun can be useful, you will do them more.

4 as Your Here-and-Now Number

You have a strong physical presence even though your demeanour may be quiet, and you may exude an earthy sex appeal. You probably make an impact on your environment – you may be the one doing the cooking and cleaning, for example, or moving the furniture. You like to use your bodily strength, not just in the sense of brute force (Four as a Here-and-Now Number does not cause you to be physically muscular), but merely to be effectual. You may also relish sport, such as cycling, jogging or power-walking.

Make it work for you

- State clearly what you want – for instance, if you need to go home on time, say so, and go
- Make the most of your physical appearance through good diet, exercise and stylish clothes
- Find a sport you can be good at – it is a marvellous outlet and will raise your 'feel-good' factor
- Enshrine some treasured possessions but, beyond those, learn that space is a commodity and treasure that

However, it is hard for you to get out of the 'back room'. If you also have numbers such as One or Five strong in your make-up, you could find it very irritating that people expect you to be predictable and you may have dreams of shocking them with some dramatic act. Yet the chances are this won't happen, as you might feel you would let yourself down – much better to get on with the washing-up and take pride in a clean kitchen.

Acquiring possessions is important to you and you may measure yourself and others by what you have. Concentrating on this too much may not further your well-being, however. It could lead to lack of self-respect, and focusing on status symbols can make your personality less interesting. If you don't feel good about yourself, you may compensate for this by wanting more stuff – and so you can get into a vicious cycle. Your mission is to enjoy material things with abandon, without putting things in control of your life. Because your identity is bound up to some extent in your possessions, you may become a hoarder. If you feel subconsciously you have lost meaning in life, holding on to stuff may seem like a way of preserving what you value, including times that are past. The great thing is you also keep your friends – and they are priceless.

You get satisfaction from proving your strength.

5 as Your Personality Number

Lively and witty, with anecdotes and jokes spilling continually, you are usually surrounded by a giggling gang. Your diary is full to overflowing, and when you arrive the mood always livens up – that is if you turn up at all. You don't mean to be unreliable, but you can be impulsive, and you hate to turn down a better offer. You change your mind like the wind and you probably don't see why you shouldn't, because there are so many different ways of looking at things and, if you hit upon a stimulating alternative viewpoint, how boring would it be not to explore it?

Being a lover of information, you are not only conversant with the latest gossip, but you also like to stay abreast of the news, the latest scientific advances, the intricacies of international politics and the plot of your favourite soap. You may have a reputation for being well informed – a 'mega-brain' even – but your knowledge might not go very deep. You quickly absorb the essentials of things, but the details might seem tedious to you. While you tend to remember what you read and hear, you don't always believe it. You are sceptical and, although many subjects fascinate you, you put your faith in few. That is fine, but remember the true

Communication is your lifeblood and you are always texting or on the net.

'sceptic' has an open mind, and is not determined to disbelieve. Social networking and text messages take up a lot of your time and you can get caught up on the internet for hours, until you get bored with sitting still. Always on the move, you like to be mobile, so you love to travel locally and further afield. Adventure is great, but you also like to look for the lively and unusual in the everyday. Your circle of friends is probably wide, and continually fluctuating. Meeting people from other cultures interests you, and you cannot get enough of new sights and experiences. While you are very interested in your fellow humans and love to interact, you rarely get emotionally close. You may be wary of having your wings clipped or getting 'heavy' – it is not your style.

Tips

- Remember to listen as well as talk – you could miss something crucial
- Some subjects are worth studying in depth – try this with something that has in-built variety and stimulation
- If you scatter your energies you will become overwrought, so remember to relax regularly
- Life is the art of asking the right questions, not relentlessly pursuing answers, so formulate your questions with care

5 as Your Life Path Number

You are on a mission to become educated, and it is very important to you to feel you know a thing or two and are learning three or four more. If you don't have the opportunity to go to university, for instance, you will probably be very discontented – having said that, you always will find a way to achieve your goals because you are resourceful and adaptable in the extreme.

You probably have several strings to your bow and it is quite possible that you can do more than one job – you could work as a journalist during the week and be an electrician at weekends. Your mind is quick and your knowledge of some subjects encyclopaedic, but you can also be deft with your hands.

Creativity is very important for you. You don't do this so much for the kudos – although you like the limelight as much as the next person – but because making something seems a kind of magic to you, and you are fascinated by the laws that govern the Universe. You want to be able to work with these and manipulate them as much as possible. Once you have completed a task, you cannot wait to get on with the next one – sometimes you can be quite casual about what you achieve because once you understand something it seems easy. However, you love to show other people the way to do it because you are a great communicator.

Being a jack-of-all-trades, whatever you do in life must produce variety and be constantly intriguing, otherwise you will not be at your best and you will feel frustrated. You could even become cranky and slightly mentally unstable if you have

To do

- Keep a journal – it is a way of capturing your wide life experience
- Sign up for short-term courses, so you have things you can complete without running out of steam
- Learn a foreign language; if you already speak one, learn another

to conform to rigid timetables and repetitive work. In life you are likely to experience many changes, so that after 20 years you may be in a completely different place, externally and internally. Always communicate – people can cope with your changeability if they know what is going on.

Famous people

- Pierre-Auguste Renoir 25.2.1841
- Che Guevara 14.6.1928
- Mick Jagger 26.7.1943
- Colin Farrell 31.5.1976

Mobile and energetic and electric, Mick Jagger is a typical 5.

5 as Your Soul Number

You have a strong urge to live life to the full. Hedonistically, you extract all the sweetness from each moment and each experience, like a bee sucking nectar. Then, like the bee, you buzz off to somewhere new. You have a deep and insatiable yearning to travel physically and emotionally, and you may be always planning trips and outings. Maybe you are an armchair traveller, nose stuck in a book while your mind ranges far and wide – but it is unlikely that your body will be able to keep still for long.

Movement is part of the fibre of your being. In fact you may enjoy dancing, because it is a way of communicating many moods, emotions and experiences by moving your body.

You love surprises and find new things thrilling. Sometimes you do mischievous things just to see what happens. You like to see how *you* will react as much as anyone else, because sometimes you amaze yourself.

Often you find you intuitively understand what people are trying to say, and you may be telepathic. However, while you are quick to tune in, you may tune out again just as swiftly, leaving the person who thought they were 'clicking' with you confused and nonplussed. You have a yearning to communicate, which may appear as a wish to be close, but actually you can be quite wary of emotional closeness because you sense it may tie you down. This applies as much to your own emotions as those of others – you know that if you get involved it could limit you in some way. Sometimes the most difficult 'communication' of all can be between your different selves – you may disregard, repress or even fear your feelings and needs. There is a paradox here, because you have a profound need for freedom and variety, but in the end this could become dry and meaningless without a dialogue with others in which you truly give of yourself. Some dedicated self-analysis would be of help to you, because by being able to communicate honestly with yourself you will be all the better able to interact with others in a way that will fulfil you. Pretending to be what you are not will make you feel trapped – don't even contemplate doing this!

A life of Five an be as unpredictable as you seem to everyone else.

Mantras and images

- A foolish consistency is the hobgoblin of little minds
- Life is about satisfying curiosity
- Variety is the spice of life
- Change is the only constant
- All part of life's rich tapestry
- Rules were made to be broken
- Have suitcase, will travel

5 as Your Destiny Number

Experience, they say, is the great teacher, and you may have a life full of ups and downs. Once may be an accident, twice carelessness – but the third time it will help if you ask yourself if, in some way, you brought about that circumstance on purpose. Are you living life on the brink, pushing things to the limit because it makes you feel alive? What are you running away from? There are ways to get high without taking risks, and there are chances you can take that can make life exciting without being destructive.

As you were growing up, there may have been some instability around. People may have escaped from their true feelings by creating melodramas. You may have become caught up in these without realizing what was happening, and you may now be repeating that pattern. But life does not have to be like that. You have a sharp and logical mind and you can use it to get yourself on an even keel.

You have a talent for understanding all sorts of things – in fact you are probably brilliant – and there may have been people in your life who relied on you to show them how things work. You may have been the brains of your family, or the one that livened things up, telling jokes around the dinner table and finding solutions to problems. From a blown fuse to a complex tax return, you have the answer – but you are not always there to give it. Places to go, people to see, here today, gone tomorrow and back the day after. It is your way of not getting tied down. But there are other ways of

Lessons to learn

- Be an opportunist in a positive and helpful way
- Leave the past behind, but don't 'throw the baby out with the bathwater'
- Work at understanding yourself and others

maintaining your liberty, so preserve your own space by doing what you are so good at – communicating clearly.

You have the gift of bringing excitement into the lives of others and you probably make more of an impact than you realize.

Little things you say and do bring a glimpse of other perspectives, inspiring ideas, exciting possibilities – creating 'light-bulb' moments in your mind and the minds of those in your orbit. Be adventurous, learn to change and be clever about what you change into.

Finding yourself where no one else has ventured can be a massive thrill.

5 as Your Here-and-Now Number

Whatever next? Your exploits keep you as 'flavour of the month' within your circle as your unpredictable behaviour surprises, entertains and keeps them guessing. You don't have to try hard – your thirst for new experience continually gets you into scrapes and adventures, but sometimes you do crazy things just for the hell of it. Who needs boring routine?

If you relax inwardly you can think on your feet and shoot from the hip.

Possibly you have a reputation for being cool. You may like to customize your clothes or at least choose outfits that are unusual and trendy. You quite like to shock, and you are not apparently bothered what other people think. This is not because you are insensitive; rather it is because you don't have time to worry about it. There is so much to interest you, and your mind gets distracted away from things that might distress others. Anyway, if one person turns the cold shoulder there are many others who will be smiling.

Unreliability is something that you may turn into an art form. Friends get used to you being an hour or more late, as you chat to everyone you meet on the way. It is not unusual for you to double-book or just not turn up. Eventually friends may get clever and tell you a start time that is an hour in advance of the real time; then you arrive on time, become bored waiting and go off somewhere that has more to offer.

Five as a Here-and-Now Number can make you feel quite uncomfortable with yourself if you have more staid numbers such as Two, Four or Eight strong in your make-up. You may not understand why you get distracted and find yourself flitting from one thing to another. Learn to trust your ingenuity, but if you relax you will be able to think on your feet and you will

surprise yourself with what you achieve. Your amazing memory can turn up spot-on facts just when they are needed. You can weigh up a situation in seconds, and have inventive, practicable solutions at your fingertips. While these may be a little quirky they move things forward. You are resourceful, adaptable, lively and buzzing with information. Why do you have a secret fear that you may be dull? Give yourself a talking to.

Make it work for you

- Several distinct groups of friends will enable you to feel easy expressing different parts of yourself
- Get into the habit of giving a 'definite maybe', so you don't let people down or feel constrained
- Indulge yourself with as many exciting exploits as you can and tell people about them, or write about them
- Try to get a column in a local newspaper or parish journal
- You may enjoy having an alter ego or two on the Internet – but don't go too far

6 as Your Personality Number

Usually on a charm offensive, you know how to spread sunshine all around. You instinctively create beauty and balance wherever you are – you are the one who stands up to tweak your friend's pictures, so they hang straight and look pleasing. As for your own home, everything is well chosen, easy on the eye and as serene as possible.

Tips

- Learn to say how you feel calmly and pleasantly – this will make for better harmony in the long term
- If you cannot make everything perfect, make one perfect room, or even a corner, on which to fix your eyes
- All forms of beauty are soothing to you, so paint your nails and wear rings and bracelets, because you will see more of your hands than your face
- 'We'll see', 'I'll let you know' and 'If possible' should be your stock phrases, so you don't over-commit
- Enjoy the gossip all you want, but always say something nice

You love people to turn up with flowers, and you probably have the patience to arrange them. At table, you make sure that everyone is served before you pick up your knife and fork, and you will steer the conversation so that it is light and bright. Politics are out, and when it comes to the gory details of someone's operation – move swiftly on.

You are probably admired for your fabulous grooming, manicured nails, coordinated outfit and not a hair out of place. Even if you are relaxing in a tracksuit, you still look attractive, because the colour will suit you and you will have remembered your jewellery. You know how to make the best of yourself, but this is more than skin deep. It is important to you to create a calm atmosphere and you will usually find a way to pour oil on troubled waters. A great peacemaker, you can generally find a purpose or topic that will unite the people you are with, and if

You have to have something attractive to look at and nails are always on show.

there are differences of opinion you are the soul of tact, easing everyone on to common ground.

Even-tempered and tolerant, you have a long fuse but you can become very stern if there is a hint of injustice, and you may stick up for the underdog. You give the image of perfection, so what is the catch? You may bottle up your feelings in the interests of harmony and sometimes these can come out in a burst of spite. Gossip is your weakness – you do love to 'dish the dirt'. Because it is so important to you to get everything right, you can sometimes be very jealous. In your own quiet way, you can be very competitive and this can cause you stress. Try to remember that no one is comparing you with anyone and you have nothing to prove.

6 as Your Life Path Number

A meaningful role in your community is essential to you, and you may well have a vocation. As a child you may have dreamed of being a doctor, nurse or teacher and, even if you don't literally take on one of those professions, an element of caring, healing and nurturing will be present in what you do.

It is not always easy for you to come to a decision, and you need to feel that what you choose is supported by the group you are in. You call meetings and have discussions, easing everyone towards consensus. You are good at seeing the big picture, and your approach is inclusive – you look for and quickly spot any common denominator. So you are a terrific asset in situations that call for diplomacy and tact. You probably feel responsible for the comfort, well-being and success of everyone around you, and you are committed and dedicated. However, sometimes you can spread yourself too thinly, trying too hard to be all things to all people. This can occasionally cause you to do the very thing you want to avoid – let someone down. Also, your love of peace means that you need to get away from it all when matters hot up, so just at the very moment you are most needed you may have slipped away to smell the roses.

To do

- Invest in one or two original works of art, especially if you know the artist – even with a modest budget they will give you joy
- Have a mini clear-out each week, even if it is only one cupboard or drawer – clutter is unaesthetic
- Find a good group to be a meaningful part of

Being a fabulous team player, you often hold the side together, not so much through your inspired leadership, but through empathy. Wherever you are, you have the ability to create a sense of family. You can turn a waiting room, common room or staff kitchen into a cosy haven, with the addition of some skilful touches.

Culture and art are very important to you. The influence of 2×3 in your nature means that you encourage others to be creative and find themselves through play. You may well be artistic yourself, but expressing yourself is not quite so important as feeling that you are surrounded by beauty and grace – it is what life is all about.

Famous people

- Francisco Goya 30.3.1746
- TS Eliot 26.9.1888
- Elisabeth Kübler-Ross 8.7.1926
- George Walker Bush 6.7.1946
- Jane Goodall 3.4.1934

6 as Your Soul Number

Beauty and tranquillity are as necessary to you as the air you breathe, and in fact without them you can become ill. However, the good thing is that you are able to see beauty where others might see only the commonplace, or even the unattractive. If there is something lovely to look at you will concentrate on that – for instance, if a single flower grows in a rubbish dump you will focus on the glory of its petals and ignore the rubbish if you possibly can.

The Chinese say 'Have nothing in your home that is neither useful nor beautiful'. You follow this as far as possible, being very aware of visual appeal. Given half a chance, your home will look like something out of a glossy magazine, and you love to go shopping for curtains, furniture and ornaments. You can create a lovely ambience with scents, candles and your own *je ne sais quoi*. Entertaining appeals to you, although you may prefer a relaxed kitchen supper to a formal dinner or wild party. Sometimes you go too far to please people, and if you have numbers like One or Five in your make-up you can drive yourself crazy with '*Why* did I agree to that?' Your soft heart may be exploited by those who take kindness for a weakness. Deeply sensitive to the problems in the world, you may find the

You love music. Use it to soothe away troubles.

news depressing. You are a champion of justice and may struggle to accept that people can be cruel to each other. It may be better to listen to music, which you probably adore and have playing most of the time anyway, when you are alone. Not that you are often solitary – you love your family, and your friends may be another 'family' as you need to be part of a caring group. You may be quite sentimental, with a collection of photos and souvenirs, all with their special memories attached. You seek solace in refined routines that give you a sense of order and balance – tea at 3pm, a scented bath before bedtime – but you should not become obsessive about these. You may long to have children, but always remember that it is the little child within you that needs love the most. When you feel secure within, your radiance will shine forth and clothe anything that is close to you with beauty.

Mantras and images

- A thing of beauty is a joy for ever
- Peace at any price – almost
- If music be the food of love, play on
- To lose oneself in something – or someone – worthwhile is the greatest bliss
- God's in His Heaven, all's right with the world
- I am part of the family of Earth

6 as Your Destiny Number

Family is key to you, in one form or another, and possibly you played an important role in your birth family as the one who smoothed things over. You may have acted as mum or dad to younger siblings while your parents were absent, or maybe you were the one who tried to make peace between your parents when they were arguing.

If there was a serious upset you would have refused to choose, maybe hoping that by being loyal to both parties you could prevent a split. If there was a divorce you may have found this especially traumatic, unless it was very well managed, trying to preserve some semblance of harmony.

Lessons to learn

- A family is made up of individuals who are being themselves – otherwise it is not a real family
- Remember that outward forms can be an illusion – don't be taken in by appearances
- Food for the body is important, but food for the soul is vital, and the best dish is unconditional love

You may try hard to keep up with your neighbours with the smartest car and the neatest garden, but it is more likely that you have deeper values and you want to appear as the perfect family. If there is such a thing as the 'perfect' family, you will be the one to create it, but it is very important that you remember a true family means everyone being able to be themselves and still be accepted. Some honest scrapping can be better than sugary pretence, which will only stir up trouble in the long term. When things go awry, you may blame yourself – this is silly because you will, in all probability, have given absolutely everything to retain family solidarity. Believing you can – and should – control such matters can be a form of egotism. Letting go and thereby preserving your own calm will be far better for everyone.

Building and maintaining a home is in your hands.

Having a home and family of your own is deeply important to you, and may well be your strongest drive. Food and nutrition are high on your priorities. You could turn into an 'alpha' mum or dad, always fighting for the best for your kids. However, you may find that your family of origin still exercises the most powerful influence and you may need to be careful that you don't turn to your parents or siblings before your partner. If you find yourself running around for your extended family while those at home are having to fend for themselves, you need to ask yourself what you are clinging to, and whom you really need to please. Learn from the past, move on from it and recreate the best of it in your own adult life – no one is better than you at creating domestic bliss.

Correctly choosing the people you need to please is crucial.

6 as Your Here-and-Now Number

You won't answer the phone before you are happy with how you look, and when you make an appearance in your designer gear you are an inspiration, not to mention a cause for envy. You probably get some secret satisfaction from that because, if you are honest, you can be insecure about your appeal and your glamorous image hides a fear of being ugly or in some way unattractive.

With a strong Six element, you may consider cosmetic surgery, and this is even more the case with Six as your Here-and-Now Number. Image is all-important, and you can even risk losing some of your identity in trying to live up to an ideal that may be essentially empty. This is an extreme scenario, however, and usually all you do is make sure that you, and everything you own, are as pleasing as possible. Why not?

By no means everything is cosmetic, however. You have a need to make everything around you as pleasant as possible on all levels. This means your favourite word may be yes – it may just pop out before you realize what is happening, so natural is it for you to go

Learn to enjoy your good looks without worrying.

Make it work for you

- Lend support only when it is asked for – there are plenty who need you
- Practise saying no to small things – it will gradually become easier to say it to bigger requests
- Keep to your most important principles so you respect yourself and earn the respect of others
- 'Doormat' is not a good look – learn when to get up and get out

with what others want. This may sound like weakness, but it is not – it just feels so much better when you 'go with the flow'. Other people may appear 'stronger', but that is probably because they are less in tune with the feelings of others and don't sense an atmosphere of disharmony. People like you are the cement that holds the group together, but you need to make sure that you don't get lost in the process.

Being a 'joiner' suits you, and you are probably good at organizing outings and trips for the group. Plush restaurants are a favourite with you and you can be a hedonist, who leads others into delicious temptation. You protect those who are vulnerable and anyone who thinks you are some kind of pushover may take a step back when bullying or unfairness make you show your teeth. However, sometimes you need to learn to keep your nose out of things and let people fight their own battles. The extent to which you develop your social conscience in a balanced and sensible way will have a big effect on your contentment. You will feel good if you can mobilize everyone to clean up the local playing field or help out at a school or an old people's home, but if you try to meddle with what is behind your neighbours' closed doors you will end up in a mess. Be wise.

7 as Your Personality Number

'Earth calling Number Seven – come in please!' Often you seem to be in a 'zone' and, even when you are giving your attention to a purpose or person, there seems to be a part of you that is not quite 'there'. You may be thinking deeply about what is going on, or you may have gone off at a tangent. It may be hard for others to understand what you are doing, or why, and you are not in a rush to explain. This could be because you enjoy being inaccessible, but more likely it is because you cannot put what is going on in your mind into words.

Tips

- Learn to meditate or some other mental discipline that will help you detach – that way you will think more clearly
- When you get fearful or morose, employ relentless logic, such as 'When in my past has "the worst" happened? Probably never'
- Find something truly worth investigating to explore – don't analyse trivia
- Develop your intuition with a subject like Tarot
- Get a good education – you will feel at your best if you are always on a course of some kind

Sometimes you look like a rabbit in the headlights and people may believe that you are going to mess up, but they are wrong. Although the way you get your results may be mysterious, you do get them, and they are usually impressive. Things have a way of 'happening' around you.

You have very high standards of performance and you can be your own worst enemy, worrying ceaselessly about 'getting it right' or trying to work out better ways of going about things. Have you ever heard the phrase 'If it ain't broke, don't fix it'? Sometimes you over-complicate your life, and you may miss the obvious as you sniff around looking for clues. However, you are very intuitive, and if you listen to that voice whispering within you it will never steer you in the wrong direction.

Daydreams can be a prelude to inspired action.

You have a gift for seeing certain things very clearly. These may be the important things, such as how a person truly feels and whether something is going to work, and your perceptions can be staggering. Magnetic and mysterious, you may fascinate some people. Others sense your depth and come to you for advice about key things in their life. At those times your insights may surprise even you, as you just 'know' certain things without being told. Psychic? Probably, but your conclusions come from your acute and sometimes subconscious observations, which may add up to be greater than the sum of their parts. When you learn to relax and trust yourself, you will be amazed at the clarity of your vision.

7 as Your Life Path Number

A seeker after wisdom, you value knowledge for its own sake but also because you know it makes you powerful. You want to have as many options as possible in life – not because you need variety and excitement precisely, but because you believe instinctively that there is safety in numbers when it comes to transferable skills.

To do

- Spend regular time alone, making sure you enjoy your own company
- Find something interesting to probe, such as your family tree
- Do crosswords and puzzles regularly – they will keep your mind supple and distract you from negative thinking

A sharp mind makes you more effectual as well as positive.

'Safety' is actually one of your goals. This is not the material safety sought by Four, or the safety in a relationship that Two focuses upon. You are looking for a security that is more profound because it involves a true understanding of how the world and the people in it tick. This understanding can give you control, of a subtle kind. Once you have knowledge, you may keep it to yourself – people may not know about your capabilities and you will only pass them on to the favoured few.

You are probably interested in the paranormal. This may be because you sense there is a whole area of potential for you to master. You have the insight and the self-discipline of the Magus, and you may enter territory that others only dream about. Or you may be determined to debunk anything you see as 'unscientific', wanting to prove that there are certain laws that existence follows and these have already been defined. In either case your single-mindedness can become obsessive, so it is vital that you create balance in your life with simple pleasures and things that you just 'feel' and 'do' without analysing.

For you to make the best of yourself, a good education is essential. This should be broad-based, giving you plenty of information so you can choose your speciality. You need mental challenge, so that your mind works positively – without this you may sometimes get depressed. You also need to follow your hunches and not fear being wrong; intuition is like a muscle – it gets stronger when you use it regularly. Sometimes you will find that you progress much better when you 'go with the flow'. It is hard for you to believe that things can come easily, but sometimes the greatest mystery of life is in contemplating the fact that they do.

Reality is not always what it seems and it is something we create, so be optimistic at all times.

Famous people

- St Teresa of Avila 28.3.1515
- Winston Churchill 30.11.1874
- Eric Clapton 30.3.1945
- Susan Sarandon 4.10.1946
- John F Kennedy 29.5.1917
- Paul Gauguin 7.6.1848

7 as Your Soul Number

The world was not really meant for souls such as yours. Reality is too banal and boring. The truth of the matter is that you are aware, in your heart, that 'reality' is not real at all, and you long to dive below the surface of life, to explore other worlds and other states of being. You may believe in fairies and aliens, and be interested in witchcraft – in fact it might suit you to have a UFO poster on your wall with the caption 'I want to believe'.

On the other hand, you may find all the enchantment you need contemplating the patterns on a leaf, or standing stock still in woodland, waiting for the badgers and deer to come out.

You probably actively seek time alone. Because you are sensitive, you may feel bombarded by sights and sounds and by the expectations and feelings of others.

Sometimes you think you would be happy if you were the last person on earth. At other times you long for intense and spellbinding contact with others. Your inner life is very vivid and your imagination is so strong that it almost makes things real. Sometimes you believe it *does* make things real. After all, what is 'real' anyway? What we see as the world is merely a construct of our brains, and what

Mantras and images

- Anything is possible
- Prayer can change the world
- The best things in life are not seen or heard – they are felt within the heart
- The divine is all around, in every bird, every tree, every flower
- In dreams begins responsibility
- As above, so below

we are truly a part of is a whirling mass of energy. Concepts like this fascinate you, and you may find them consoling when it all gets too much.

Your privacy is vital to you and if it is invaded you may become overwrought and agitated. You should never be forced into a role of someone else's choosing – it is deeply damaging to you not to have your views respected. Inside, you are quite fragile and you may protect this fragility by keeping yourself to yourself. This does not always work well for you, and you may be accused of being 'stuck up'. If you have more extrovert or friendly numbers strong in you, such as Three or Six, you may feel ashamed of your need to withdraw, but it is therapeutic and strengthening. The beauties of Nature make your heart sing, and one of the most touching manifestations of your sensitivity may be your care for wildlife.

Time to contact your inner wise person is vital for Seven.

7 as Your Destiny Number

Your environment has probably always contained some kind of a puzzle. As you grew up you may not have felt quite sure what was going on. There may have been skeletons in the cupboards, or your parents may have actively concealed information from you in order to protect you. More likely you were just extra aware of undercurrents. These may sometimes have upset you, because you may have feared they threatened your security.

Now you make it your business to be one jump ahead, so you can protect you and yours from hidden threats. Often you are on the right track and you prove time and time again that you have seen things correctly; it is very hard to pull the wool over your eyes. At other times you may be a little paranoid – there is no need to be.

Your destiny will take you along the 'road less travelled'. Even if you do something quite mundane, and your life looks pretty average, scratch just below the surface and there will be a flavour of the original. You may be in possession of some secret that you have to protect, and you may feel that you have been entrusted with responsibilities that others would never understand. You probably are something of a loner. You work towards long-term goals that may take many years to reach, and you keep your plans secret – you may

fear that if others know about them they might ridicule or obstruct. Often people are truly surprised by you, when you achieve something amazing or do something totally wacky.

An 'alternative' lifestyle may appeal – it may be easier to follow your star if you 'drop out', and in extreme cases you may take to the road in a motorhome or live in a tent in a field. At times you become a hermit. You may reinvent yourself and re-emerge on the scene with an entirely different image. People are fascinated by you and believe you have some secret that no one else is privy to. In their most difficult hour you come up trumps, with an answer or a course of action that no one else would ever have dreamed about.

You may take to the road or dream of living in a forest.

Lessons to learn

- You must stop imagining the worst – imagining the best will enable you to create it
- Ensure that your goals have deep meaning – you invest so much in them and they should not merely be about control or self-aggrandizement
- Faith can move mountains

7 as Your Here-and-Now Number

What is going on behind those smokescreens? Your friends imagine all sorts of things, but you rarely give anything away. This may be because there is little to reveal when you get down to it. If the rest of your nature is made up of Twos and Fours, for instance, you may be more concerned with what is for dinner (and with whom you are having it) than you are about the meaning of life.

However, Seven as your Here-and-Now Number is bound to make you just a little spooky – in the nicest possible way. The way you act is a trifle unusual, and you are unpredictable – even quite shocking. You are capable of speaking out loud the very thing everyone is thinking but did not like to say.

Explaining yourself could be a struggle, especially when it comes to your feelings, and however earnestly you try you may still be misunderstood. But sometimes you don't see why you should expose yourself and you may give way to a tantrum. You may believe that people should realize a few things without having them spelt out.

Make it work for you

- If you really do want to keep your feelings private, put a cheerful face on it – moods will give the game away, or at least reveal the fact that there is a game
- Trust begets trust – you may have to give away a bit more about yourself if you are to find out the truth about others
- Learn sometimes to accept, without understanding – for instance, love makes no sense, but where would we be without it?
- Be careful what you wish for – it will probably manifest, and you could be stuck with it

Never one to wear your heart on your sleeve, anyone who is told something in confidence by you is honoured. A loyal friend yourself, you expect the highest standards from your friends. You are very sensitive, really tuned in to what other people think about you, and others may have no idea how their opinions are affecting you. You sense the mood of the crowd, and it changes your own state of mind. Sometimes the 'vibes' are so hard to deal with that you just have to go off on your own. Learning how to cleanse yourself spiritually will be worth the effort.

Role-playing probably appeals and it may be you who dresses up in a bandana and hoop earrings to be the gypsy fortune-teller at the local fete. You may lose yourself in

daydreams and you may become quite addicted to escapist films and novels, from sci-fi to romance – the crazier the better. When you realize that focusing on something really does make it happen in your life, you may have great fun manifesting what you want. Sometimes, however, you find that what you desired so hotly is not that great in reality, so it is important to focus your concentration on things that are going to be of long-term benefit and greater significance.

Life is a mystery. Immerse yourself in all its intricacies.

Assets and power are your currency and you use them well.

8 as Your Personality Number

From your designer labels to your sweeping body language, something about you says 'notice me – I'm important'. You probably feel it is up to you to take control, and challenges bring out the best in you. Like Four, you are extremely practical, but you have a wider vision and organizing on a large scale is natural to you. Like One, you are a leader, but you don't charge off into the blue all fired up and impatient – you make sure that you have your route planned and that people are indeed going to be following you.

You are capable of management at work and in your leisure – for instance, you would be a fabulous asset helping a friend plan their wedding, and you would not be frightened by the complications of cake, dress and seating plans. In fact with your excellent 'money head', you would have the entire event costed and budgeted, getting the best deal with a few perks thrown in. Telling people what to do is not a problem for you – you can behave like the Chief Executive Officer of a multinational company (indeed, one day you may *be* such a CEO) and people instinctively give you respect. Charming and confident, as long as you avoid any hint of the autocratic, you can get the best out of people. However, you may struggle

Tips

- Remember that you only become rich by enriching others in some way – that may include giving them responsibilities
- Power 'to', not power 'over', should be your goal
- Settle for being 'sainted in moderation' for true achievements rather than placed on a pedestal from which the only way is down
- Always have a nest egg that you don't risk, no matter what

with delegating, because few people come up to your standards, and if you are not careful you can get depleted trying to be 'chief cook and bottle-washer' at the same time.

Among your friends you like to be influential – top of the guest list or playing a significant role. You also like to be recognized for your success and probably your wealth. If your personality is functioning positively, you will undoubtedly be very prosperous because you have an instinct for investments and the main chance. However, your pride won't let you admit to weakness, and if things go wrong you find it almost impossible to ask for help. Struggling on alone, with a smile on your face, you could be facing bankruptcy or the loss of your home or business, but no one would guess. Luckily your acumen usually saves the day and you can rise like a phoenix from the ashes.

The sky's the limit when you are truly expressing yourself.

8 as Your Life Path Number

The will to power is strong within you, and you have a relentless drive for material security, breadth of choice and scope for effective action. You are probably very aware of power structures in the collective – big business, society at large and also closer to home. Instinctively, you will know who makes the decisions and why, and, in any area that interests you, you will progress at a steady rate.

You may judge yourself and others by your possessions – try not to do this, for it can be a distraction. It could even be your downfall. If you try to get too much too quickly, you could overstretch yourself financially and in other ways. Rest assured that if you take your time and build a solid foundation, you will achieve success. Status is vital to you.

This is not a petty 'keeping up with the neighbours' – it is about making constructive change in the world. However, if you don't have some real standing, you might be tempted to take short cuts in order to make an impression. An extreme example of this could be the person who lives in a mansion on which they cannot pay the mortgage, or who runs up massive expenses, flashing cash and stretching plastic and putting off the inevitable day of reckoning. Really you are too sensible for that.

Driven and determined, you take yourself very seriously. Sometimes others may find you overpowering, which is a strange thing, because deep within you are very conscious of the potency of others and often feel at a disadvantage. Being competitive and hierarchical, you have

To do

- Train yourself in business and finance – pick a sensible course to study
- Look closely at the life and philosophy of your favourite successful person – note what you can learn from them
- Create a five-year game-plan and review it regularly

your eyes on the top job and may want to dislodge its occupant. By the same token, you may feel threatened by challenges from peers and inferiors. It is important that you nurture a strong self-esteem with a realistic sense of your capabilities and a tolerance and appreciation of fellow humans – in this way you will get ahead brilliantly. You are destined for some kind of managerial post and may even become a tycoon. However, it may be better for you to be a big fish in a small pond, rather than to head for the open sea, which may be shark-infested. In the end, you need to find a stronger power within you, and to find spiritual meaning in what you do, so that your achievements enrich you on all levels.

Focusing your ambition in a way that helps all concerned will satisfy you.

8 as Your Soul Number

Making an impact, making a difference – this is naturally you, and if you cannot be of some importance something within you shrivels. However, if you listen to the promptings of your intuition, you will know instinctively which path leads to the bright lights and limousines. You have a ruthless ambition and can keep to your course no matter what, but this may be anything but obvious to others, and one of your strengths may be that you catch people off guard. One day they may describe you as an 'overnight success' when you have been beavering away for years.

Material security and the finer things of life are balm to your soul. However, that does not mean you are fundamentally materialistic. You are aware of the ability of practical comforts to set you free and give you time and choice. If you don't have to worry about where the next mouthful is coming from, you have the chance to accomplish so many other things. By successfully getting to grips with the world you come to realize that the ultimate mastery is control over yourself. You may develop a will of iron, but when you realize that imagination is always

Mantras and images

- I am building my life brick by brick
- Onwards and upwards
- The secret of success is being constant to my purpose
- True power is power over myself
- My will walks hand in hand with my imagination
- I am like a mighty tree: deep roots, strong trunk, far-reaching branches
- I am a force to be reckoned with

Your art of dreaming possible dreams makes you a winner.

stronger than willpower you put effort into directing your fantasies, so you can reshape your life.

One of your greatest challenges is that of letting go of the control of those you care about. Often you can see so clearly what needs to be done and you know how to do it. It is unbelievably hard to have to stand by and watch those you love make mistakes and even hurt themselves, and you may have to bite your tongue on 'I told you so'. It is important to realize that you have done your best and try not to dominate. Sometimes the greatest gift you can give to people is the freedom to make their own mistakes – and of course it always helps when you are there to pick up the pieces.

8 as Your Destiny Number

As you were growing up, power and status were probably an issue for you and for those around you. Your family may have felt in some way disadvantaged and that they had to fight for their position, or somehow looked down upon. Or it may have been that your family were influential, with an image and status to uphold. This will have left you with a sense of responsibility and maybe a sense of mission. It may seem up to you to make good, and you may feel quite burdened by this. However, concrete achievements will give you your greatest pleasure and satisfaction.

Possibly you are quite scheming and you may have a schedule for your life, with many of the details and timescales laid out. To your credit, you usually achieve what you set out to do. Your strength of character is remarkable and people tend to follow you because you command respect. It is important to use this wisely and not to become bullying or aggressive.

It is likely that you have a 'Type A' personality and you can push yourself beyond the limit of your endurance. Whatever you achieve, you may never be satisfied and always want to do more, have more, be more. It may seem to everyone around you as if you have 'made it', but you still want something bigger and better. If you exhaust yourself you may become depressed. It is also a shame not to stop and appreciate what you have. How many shoes can one person wear? And how many rooms do you really need before you feel you have come 'home'? In the end you realize that you 'cannot take it with you' and that the most enduring legacy you can leave is that of generosity and kindness.

Lessons to learn

- Failure may be tough, but not even trying is far worse in the long run – failure will only make you stronger, so be brave
- Enough is as good as a feast
- People will follow you for what you *are* rather than what you *do*, so have faith in yourself

You may do everything you can to avoid failing at anything, which is fine when it means – as it usually does – that you put 100 per cent into everything you do. But sometimes your fears get the better of you, and you may simply not go for that promotion or put in for that exam. Losing face is a nightmare for you, but you have to 'be in it to win it' and you must be aware that depriving yourself of a chance is the greatest failure of all. Remember that *all* successful people have failed many, many times, and what sets the winners apart from the losers is learning from mistakes.

Success gives you a high but doing your best is also satisfying.

8 as Your Here-and-Now Number

Why do you always have so much to do? And why is it that however much you accomplish there is always something else? It is said that if you want something done you should ask a busy person, and everyone seems to ask you. Like the man in the Greek myth, you keep rolling the stone all the way up the slope only to find that it trundles to the bottom again, and you have to start the task once more.

Make it work for you

- Showing off cheapens you – let your dignity and authority speak for themselves
- Never compare yourself to others – your worth is indisputable and you don't have to compete
- Admitting when you cannot do something is a sign of maturity and common sense
- If you want excellence, concentrate on a manageable area

Maybe you could pause to ask yourself why you let the buck stop with you? You don't have to be responsible. For some reason you may feel guilty if things are not right and you are a perfectionist, but sometimes you need to put your blinkers on and say 'not my problem'.

Creating a good impression is paramount and you may power-dress or give an impression of wealth with a subtle flash of your expensive watch. You have great taste, but sometimes you tend to dominate your company. If you let other people get a word in edgeways, they will think better of you and you will be in a stronger position, because you will know more about what makes those around you tick.

Relax and make a good impression – that will give you power.

If you are honest, at times you bite off more than you can chew, and this can be very scary because you hate the thought of letting yourself down. If you feel you are in too deep it is much better to own up. Asking for help is a sign of courage and strength, not weakness, and it will gain you greater respect in the long run.

You probably are something of a 'mega-brain' and your friends may come to you to be told how to do things. When it comes to sensible advice and sound knowledge you are second to none, but if you really don't know then never pretend. If you are found out, you will feel terrible. It is far better to say 'I'm not sure but I'll find out for you'; then you may learn something that could come in useful in the future.

9 as Your Personality Number

The wise and the open-minded, the dumped and the redundant, lost souls and lonely hearts – they all beat a path to your door. In earlier times you might have been the village wise-woman or the travelling preacher. Subconsciously you hold within you the experience of all the other eight numbers, and so you are able to understand just about anything a human being can feel and do.

'Tout comprendre, c'est tout pardonner' ('to understand everything is to forgive everything') goes the French saying, and you are very liberal in your outlook, wanting to see the best in everyone and to enable them to find it themselves. Yes, you can be a bit of a 'Pollyanna', but your optimism is usually justified, for you have a way of bringing out the best in people.

You can also give them hope – you unfurl the silver lining, put problems in perspective and suggest the spiritual meaning behind it all.

People may assume that you have your own life all sorted out, and you probably do give that impression. You hold your head high and you stand out from the

Tips

- Have a list of wise sayings that you can refer to when things seem bleak
- Sometimes you may have to be patient and wait – have faith that new meanings and fresh inspiration will find you
- It is not written anywhere that you have to be better than everyone else, so just be yourself
- Being involved in something greater than yourself will bring you ultimate satisfaction

crowd – there is a poise in your style and bearing. Optimistic, idealistic and full of fun, you often seem to be on the track of some dream, and you are vibrant and passionately involved in life. However, sometimes you just don't quite 'connect'. The 'small print' bedevils you and occasionally you are naïve – or at least suspend disbelief. You have an urgent need for fulfilment and deep inside you can get very depressed if you feel you are not achieving. Although you may inspire others and help them to believe both in themselves and in a greater power, you may struggle through a 'dark night of the soul' when your faith deserts you.

Occasionally another side of you takes over and you can be cynical and negative – 'been there, done that, got the T-shirt'. Then nothing in life seems worth the effort, and you can become bored with and critical of yourself and everyone else. At times like that it may be better not to force the issue. If you try to enjoy whatever is close at hand, you will soon find inspiration and be off once more on a voyage of discovery.

You often know best, but be prepared to learn, as well.

9 as Your Life Path Number

You are on a quest for truth, whatever that may be – and indeed the nature of 'truth' itself may be something you reflect on. Your path is that of the teacher and philosopher, and you may be working your way towards letting go of personal attachments, because you know deep inside that you are 'meant' to do something for the collective.

Of course, this does not mean that you cannot or will not get close to people and have the same kind of life as everyone else. But you cannot be too tied to the mundane or the trivial, and there will be times when your personal concerns have to take second place as you do things for the greater good of humankind and the planet.

Brigitte Bardot shows her devotion to animal rights.

Subconsciously you have a strong and wide connection to all that humanity has wrought and experienced down the ages, and you feel in some way responsible for this. You may feel drawn to making profound changes and even to becoming a spiritual leader. Charities, humanitarian and environmental causes, and some-times political matters may absorb you, and you may get up on your soapbox to bring your message of reform to the world. You can be very unselfish, but everything has its flip side, and a strain of egotism could emerge in fanatical or dogmatic views. Liberty for all may be high on your agenda, but you may struggle to give 'liberty' to anyone who disagrees with you and your version of 'the truth'.

Your sense of mission is galvanic and you can be very determined. Because of your deep knowledge of human nature, you know how to motivate the collective and you may be good at getting publicity in the media or at persuading famous people and influential people to back your cause – it is a lucky person or purpose that has you in their corner, because you put your soul and your passionate belief behind them, dedicated to ultimate success. You have a massive amount to offer the world, but it is very important that you don't lose touch with your own 'ordinariness' – you may fear this will drag you down, but it will enrich you, and a family birthday party may matter more than a political rally. Love is the strongest energy of all.

Famous people

- Albert Schweitzer 14.1.1875
- Carl Gustav Jung 26.7.1875
- Charles Lindbergh 4.2.1902
- Brigitte Bardot 28.9.1934

To do

- Find a worthwhile cause to champion – remember you can always change this at some future date
- Choose good, consciousness-raising books, and always have one by your bedside
- Try to go abroad once a year to mingle with people from other cultures

9 as Your Soul Number

You hear the music of the spheres and the cry of every orphaned child in the world. Sometimes your awareness of suffering is overwhelming and you want to rush and give away everything you have to help the starving millions – you could be the classic 'bleeding heart'. At other times you are delighted with the sheer wonder of life, with all its colour and scope, and the opportunity for happiness that is available to everyone, if we will only just open our eyes on the spiritual perspectives.

You may be drawn to the peace of ashrams, monasteries and churches, because they answer a deep need in you. You are probably religious in some way, but even if you have no specific belief you are aware of the spiritual dimension. Possibly you can be a bit prudish at times, and may inwardly shrink when your friends are too explicit about their sex lives or intimate experiences such as childbirth.

It is not that you see anything wrong with the human body, but you feel that something is missing or distorted when spirituality is left out of the picture. Sexually you may be very passionate, but you don't like to be brought down to earth – for instance 'talking dirty' could be a turn-off. You want to be lifted to the celestial heights on an emotional high instead.

Mantras and images

- Love makes the world go round
- I am watched over by angels
- My consciousness takes flight among the stars
- The more I give of myself the more I have
- It is more blessed to travel than to arrive
- There is always a rainbow
- We all carry a spark of the divine

Culture and the arts are very important to you, and music can transport you into another world. You have a secret yearning to be an exceptional artist and, if more mundane numbers such as Four and Eight are strong in your make-up, you may feel that your genuine creativity is stifled. You need to value anything creative that you produce as unique and carrying the divine spark, because if you compare yourself to the great masters you may become lost in

You need to be lifted out of the commonplace in all you do.

a black despair. This is not about being competitive (although you do have a powerful longing to be 'special') – it is about being able to reach a cosmic high. Your spiritual source constantly beckons you and you search ceaselessly for flashes of divine light that can carry you towards it.

201

9 as Your Destiny Number

Your family of origin may have been special in some way, or at least believed they were. This may be because of exceptional creativity, intelligence or public service, or because they were active in the local religious community. Possibly they had a different, or more intense, commitment, to a code of belief. There may have been a family tradition that you were expected to carry on, and the very highest standards were probably expected of you, in some sphere.

Somewhere inside you is the conviction that it is up to you to set a good example. Good manners may be very important, and you may have little patience when people are inconsiderate or too informal. You are a model of courtesy and consideration, and you may act as a guide and mentor to others. As you were growing up, people may have remarked that you had 'an old head on young shoulders', and older family members may have looked to you for advice. You probably have faith in your insight and you are extremely perceptive, able to lift people out of their petty concerns and fears and into a position of clarity.

You have a sense of hierarchy and bettering yourself is key. Education is vital to you, but this is more than academic training or learning new skills – you seek knowledge that is going to expand your perspectives. Your home may be a haven for writers, intellectuals, foreign students and representatives of spiritual disciplines, and you are very eclectic. Books are essential to you, and you may like to run your home life differently from others –

Finding out new things and accessing knowledge will always motivate you.

perhaps following Rudolph Steiner's ideas, keeping television to a minimum or being extremely environment-friendly so you recycle just about everything. You may have a shrine in your home or insist on some religious observance – or you may be deeply anti-religion, so that science or humanism become a type of 'religion'. Whatever the case, it is important to you that you create a way of life that is apart from the common herd, because you don't want to fall into unconscious living. This may make you seem snobbish, but to you life is about extending beyond the ordinary and everyday – it is people like you who brought us out of the caves and showed us the stars.

Lessons to learn

- Love your fellow humans rather than look down on them – that is the way to lift them
- Develop your creativity, even if it falls below your standards of excellence
- Give for the joy of giving, not because it enhances you in some way

9 as Your Here-and-Now Number

Rattling a collecting tin or clearing rubbish from the park, you are usually to be found doing good works of some kind. Taking a leadership role in the local community comes easily to you, and you may run for the parish council, or chair a committee set up to help and improve communal life. You could be a help in the village church, organize a pagan gathering or set up a consciousness-raising group – you are probably known as someone who is high-minded and you take great satisfaction in that.

There are those who may call you a 'know-it-all', but you probably dismiss them as 'just jealous' or simply beneath your notice. However, you are usually too wise to say this.

Although you have more than your share of wisdom and strength of character, you often find yourself agreeing with your friends against your better judgement. This is because you empathize with everyone's point of view – after all, there are as many ways of looking at things as there are people. Because of this you can sometimes find yourself in a compromising position.

This is when you need to go off on your own and find out what you truly believe. Once you feel more sure of this you can usually negotiate your way forwards and retain everyone's respect, which is essential to you. You need very much to be special – a 'cut above'. Not that you bother keeping up with the neighbours – their ethics matter more to you than their new extension. You can be a little judgemental at times. Try not to think this way, because you of all people know quite well that there are many reasons for how individuals react. You should also try not to judge yourself.

Life to you seems very exciting and you are very enthusiastic about lots of things. Most things about you are excellent; your clothes have style and you have a certain charisma. Others often admire the way you live and the things you do, and feel that you naturally stand out from the crowd. You may not agree – you fear mediocrity and the ordinary suffocates you. Give yourself credit.

You love to be a part of something that improves the world.

Make it work for you

- Ensure the things you get involved with offer you something on a personal level, or you could find that your well runs dry
- Your best is good enough
- Be aware how many times you think 'I should' or 'I ought' – who says so? Set yourself free
- Earmark times to be alone, connecting with your spirituality

Numbers 11 and 22

These two Master Numbers (see pages 60–67) will also have the characteristics of Two and Four, respectively. Master Numbers operate on a higher octave, and not everyone will respond to their call. If you find them in your make-up, you may have a choice. Do you want this extra responsibility? The paths of Eleven and Twenty-Two may not be easy, but they can be rewarding. They are felt most strongly as Personality Numbers.

11 as your Personality Number

A good listener, you listen with your heart as well as your ears and you are very intuitive. You have healing gifts – just your presence can be soothing although you may never feel you have done enough. Sensitive and excitable, you pick things up subliminally and may not always know

where a feeling has come from. Try to calm down and honour your instincts without getting carried away. Deep inside, you feel you were put on this earth to do something, and you have high expectations of yourself. There may be something of the martyr in you, which does not mean that you have a 'victim personality' (although there may be a grain of this sometimes), but it does mean that you may be willing to lose yourself in a good cause. Sometimes you come to a grinding halt, however, because you feel your best is not good enough. Remember that you don't have to save the world, and every little thing you do counts.

11 as your Life Path Number

It is relatively unusual for a Life Path Number of Two *not* to reduce to Eleven first, but your Eleven energies are available to you, lifting you above the more personal orbit of Two into the collective calling of Eleven. So don't obsess over trivial matters. Always place your ambitions in the widest context possible and think of humanity as your partner, and you can achieve great things.

Your inner truth will guide you when expressing your Master Number.

11 as your Soul Number

Identifying with an Eleven Soul Number means that you may relate to your dreams rather than to real people or the world as it is, and you may yearn for a cause that is bigger than you in which you can lose yourself. You need a meaningful spiritual path into which you can pour your zeal.

Tips

- Listen to your inner voice to find your mission
- Remember truth has many faces, and your truth may not match everyone else's

To do

- Search within yourself for a special talent

Mantra

- If you don't have a dream, how can you have a dream come true?

Eleven can encourage you to make family the first priority in life.

11 as your Destiny Number

Responding to Eleven as your Destiny Number you may make great sacrifices for your family, and you may see the human race as 'family'. You want to wake people up and help them to see a wider reality. Because your vision is so clear, you may become zealous and dogmatic, but your calling is to awaken people to their own vision, not to impose your own.

Lessons to learn

- To retain the spirit of the law, not the letter

Make it work for you

- Forge a strong relationship with your spiritual source (through prayer, meditation, ritual or whatever seems right)

11 as your Here-and-Now Number

You may be seen as the one with a message and people may respect you for your spirituality or just think you are in a 'zone'. Sometimes it may disappoint you that people seem so unaware of deeper truths, but you are doing more good than you realize.

22 as your Personality Number

Others may lose focus, but you are able to find a way through the boring details and lay the foundations for something of value. You feel it is up to you to build for the future, not for yourself but for others. You are extremely practical but your strong awareness of the feelings and needs of others can mean that your path is a hard one, because you know that some sacrifices have to be made for the good of the whole, and that the needs of the many may outweigh the wishes of the few. Patient and painstaking, you take life step by step, never losing sight of where you are going. However, while you are being strong for everyone else, sometimes you lose your own footing, and your personal life may suffer. Never forget that you also have needs and, if you are to be effectual, these must be met before anything else.

22 as your Life Path Number

Attuning to the energies of Twenty-Two lifts you beyond the scope of day-to-day work, so central to Four, and brings what you achieve into a much wider arena. Even if you are still a cog in a wheel, it needs to be a big wheel. So, for instance, your Twenty-Two Life Path could make you a scientific pioneer, but if not you will get great fulfilment from working in the lab of a pioneer, at the cutting edge of your field, getting concrete but far-reaching results.

Tips

- Life is the art of the possible – start with that
- Practicality starts with looking after yourself

To do

- Make sure your efforts go towards something meaningful – *don't* talk yourself out of this

Mantra

- Great oaks grow from small acorns

22 as your Soul Number

You long for real power to change the world and you dream of building a Utopia; you know this is possible and you can even see how it could be done. You see yourself as a practical idealist. Petty things can really upset you, however. Concentrating on a specific goal will stop you becoming overwrought.

22 as your Destiny Number

As a child you may have had to take on great responsibility for the lives of those close to you. Even if this was not the case, you will have been aware of the bigger picture, of just how much work goes into achieving what is worthwhile. It is vital for you to acquire transferable skills so you can make a difference in as wide a field as possible. Being made redundant would be a disaster for you, but that is very unlikely since you are supremely capable and resourceful.

22 as your Here-and-now number

Only fairly long names such as 'Horatio' will yield a Here-and-Now Number of Twenty-Two. If this is you, then you are often involved in some master plan, organizing something for people on a large scale. You may be regarded as a wonder-worker, but also taken for granted because it is hard for others to appreciate the scope of your achievements.

Lessons to learn

- To acquire the right skills to turn your visions into reality

Make it work for you

- Don't waste your talents – forget the office party and do the charity project

Twenty-two can make you dedicate your life to practical advantage.

4: Correspondences

Each number has certain concrete connections with the material world. These substances have a vibration that harmonises and can help a number to be expressed, and bring out its best. Any of the substances can be used for any formula – just concentrate on what you want. You can also use the correspondences to put you in touch with a number you lack.

Correspondences for Number 1

All one correspondences will boost drive, independence and initiative. Top tips: pictures of sunflowers will make a One soul radiate happiness. Wearing a red or orange gives a one personality maximum impact.

Crystals

• CARNELIAN This will help you to overcome any feelings of doubt and negativity. At the same time, this stone encourages peace and harmony and can help you relate to others while retaining your special drive. Wear it as a ring on your forefinger, for extra impact.

Sunflower has properties that mirror this cheerful flower's appearance.

• AMBER The warmth of amber will help you to express your talents with your natural confidence. If you feel under pressure, or that your efforts lack focus, light a candle and sit on the floor beside it. Take a handful of amber tumble-stones and place them around you, so that you and the candle are enclosed in a circle. Close your eyes and imagine your energy and concentration building, until you feel strong and immune from outside pressure. Keep your tumble-stones and repeat as necessary.

Flowers
• SUNFLOWER It is said that if you cut a sunflower before sunset and make a wish, it will come true before the next sunset. This cheery plant makes you feel anything is possible. Eat the seeds to be inspired.
• CARNATION Red carnations are best for healing both mind and body and bringing strength.

Herbs, trees, oils and resins
• ST JOHN'S WORT This will keep the blues at bay. You can drink it as a tea, but if any part of the herb is placed beneath your pillow it is said to enable you to dream of your future.
• ORANGE The Chinese consider oranges to be a symbol of good luck. The fragrance of essential oil of orange is one

Lucky orange will cheer you up.

of the most heartening scents. Orange pips can bring you answers, according to tradition. Think of a yes/no question you would like answered while you eat your orange. Count the seeds – if they are an even number, the answer is no; if an odd number, then it is yes.

Colours
• Red brings you the energy you need to fulfil your ambitions.
• Orange is a great colour for you, as it is very cheerful and outgoing – wear it as terracotta or peach if you find the true shade is too brash.
• Strong contrasts and bright colours in general are best for your personality.

Correspondences for Number 2

All two correspondences will enhance harmony and co-operation. Top tips: sapphire will bring out the best of two in any place. Lemon balm in the home cleanses negativity.

Crystals

• MOONSTONE Gentle moonstone brings harmony between lovers and will be beneficial for your relationships. It will also protect that sensitive nature of yours and keep you safe. Place moonstone beneath your pillow to make sure you leave your worries behind and sleep peacefully.

• SAPPHIRE This is a stone of wisdom that will help you keep things in perspective. Blue sapphire will raise your mind above petty things and will encourage you to express yourself calmly and effectively. Green sapphire will help you understand others. Pink sapphire will draw what you desire into your life and enable you to cope positively with your emotions.

Flowers

• LILY Lilies planted in the garden are said to keep unwanted visitors at bay, lifting you out of the 'gossip zone'. The first white lily of the season is said to bring strength.

• JASMINE Dried jasmine, when carried, will attract love of a deep and meaningful kind (as opposed to lust). Heat oil of jasmine to purify the air so that you can meditate or reflect with a clear head.

Herbs, trees, oils and resins

• LEMON BALM Soak a sprig of this herb in wine or juice and then share the drink with a friend or lover to strengthen and purify the bond between you. The essential oil is great for soothing nerves and panic attacks and lifting depression.

• WILLOW Traditionally, all parts of the willow tree are protective against negativity. Knock on the willow tree ('knock on wood') for good luck. An old custom states that if you want to know if you will find a partner within the next year, throw your shoe into a willow on New Year's Eve. If the shoe catches, the answer is 'yes'

Sapphire
(green)

(you are allowed nine chances at this!). Use willow baskets to feel that your life is under control.

Colours

• Silver emphasizes your receptivity, and all forms of grey will bring out your subtlety and discrimination.

• Shades of blue, turquoise and green can keep you calm and detached and emphasize your best qualities of serenity and caring.

• Soft colours and pastels harmonize with your thoughtful and gentle approach.

Lilies are valued in many esoteric areas.

Correspondences for Number 3

All Three correspondences stimulate creativity and zest for life.
Top tips: sage can stop a three personality going hyper while honeysuckle
can free a Three soul.

Citrine

Crystals

• RUBY Warm-hearted ruby will enhance your enthusiasm for life and keep you positive, so you make a good impression. It will also encourage you to follow your heart. Wearing a ruby will make you joyful. If you feel depleted, place three uncut rubies around a red candle, light the candle and feel the power of the rubies energizing you. Keep the rubies with you when you need stamina.

• CITRINE Happy citrine will help you get a good night's sleep if placed beneath your pillow. It may also stimulate psychic awareness, enabling you to still the mental chatter and focus. Wear it on your fingers or at your throat, preferably in contact with your skin, to bring you extra energy. It can also help you overcome your reluctance to commit, where that is misplaced.

Flowers

• DANDELION Cheerful and irrepressible, the dandelion is associated with many folk customs. To send a message to a loved one, blow the seedhead in his or her direction while you visualize what you want to convey. A tea made from the root can help you calm your mind and access your intuition.

• HONEYSUCKLE This sweet-smelling rambling plant is believed to bring protection, money and psychic powers. Grown near your home, it will strengthen your luck. Crush some fresh flowers against your forehead to relax and see things clearly.

Herbs, trees, oils and resins

- SAGE When carried, sage encourages wisdom. To make a wish come true, write it on a sage leaf and put it underneath your pillow for three nights running. If you dream of what you want, it will come true. If not, bury the leaf and start again.
- CLOVE Heat oil of clove to cleanse and enrich the atmosphere. Carry a clove or two about your person to attract the opposite sex – the scent (which should not be obvious) acts as an aphrodisiac.

Colours

- Yellow uplifts you, keeping your mind sharp and positive. The acid shades are best avoided, however, so think mellow. Gold is even better, adding to your natural radiance.
- Turquoise gives depth to your creativity and puts you in touch with peace and beauty.
- Anything sparkling or shimmering harmonizes with your lively personality.

Sage is valued for truth-bringing properties.

Correspondences for Number 4

All Four correspondences help practicality and achievement.
Top tips: obsidian can stop you getting bogged down in details.
The scent of patchouli gives depth to a Four personality.

Crystals

• OBSIDIAN This is a wonderful stone to make you grounded and give you protection. It is also a stone of peace. If you look deep into obsidian, it can help you get in touch with your spiritual side and the messages of your subconscious. If you need to get your life in order, take two small pieces of obsidian and place them under your bare feet, close your eyes, calm down and visualize things sorting themselves out.

• JASPER This stone brings health, beauty, healing and protection. Carry it with you if you feel challenged. Brown jasper is especially good for keeping your feet on the ground. Ring a green candle with green jasper tumble-stones and visualize yourself (or another person) as totally healthy, in order to bring healing.

Flowers

• PANSY The pansy will draw affection to you and soften the demands you feel. Plant pansies in the shape of a heart to attract romance.

• MIMOSA Scatter mimosa around any area you would like cleansed, so your mind and spirit can feel free. Bathing with mimosa in your water will destroy negativity and protect you from its return.

Herbs, trees, oils and resins

• PATCHOULI The earthy scent of patchouli awakens your sensual side and increases your sex appeal. Patchouli heated in an oil diffuser can bring you back to basics, centring your thoughts on the here and now and putting things in perspective.

Mimosa flowers – cleansing of negativity.

• CYPRESS Grown near the home, cypress is protective. The scent of cypress essential oil eases grief and negative emotions – if you need a good cry, this scent will enable your feelings to flow so you can move on.

Colours
• Brown brings out your practical side, but it also enhances the subtle style and physical ease that are your characteristics.
• The soothing qualities of most shades of green emphasize your creativity and heal stresses and strains.
• You may feel more at ease in darker colours, but accents of lighter shades will lift your spirits.

Correspondences for Number 5

Five correspondences aid communication and keep things lively.
Top tips: wearing agate can keep you on your Five life path. Blue will help
your Five here-and-now stay focused.

Crystals

• AVENTURINE This can sharpen your perceptions, increase your intelligence and make you more creative. Carry it with you for luck. Hold it between your palms to calm your emotions and enable you to express and process them.

• AGATE You can use a large piece of agate as a crystal ball. Look deep within and your thoughts will clarify, bringing you the answers you need. Wearing agate can help you speak truthfully and convey your meaning clearly. Surround a piece of blue lace agate with blue candles, to de-stress the atmosphere and enable all to have their say without argument. Keep blue lace agate on your desk, to help you to stay calm.

Blue lace
agate

Flowers

• LAVENDER This is a wonderful all-purpose scent to take away anxiety and clear the head. Take a sprig of lavender into exams or tests to keep your mind on track and bring you luck. Lavender essential oil can be heated in a diffuser to create peace and harmony. It can also be dabbed neat directly on to the skin to ease irritation.

• LILY OF THE VALLEY This can improve the memory. When placed in a room, this sweet bloom lifts everyone's spirits and brings happiness.

Herbs, trees, oils and resins

• FENNEL This was considered a protective herb to have in the home. Fennel tea soothes the digestion, which can become disturbed if your mind is turbulent, or you are dashing about. Carry a sachet of fennel seeds with you to ward off any negative thoughts.

• PEPPERMINT In earlier times this was used for healing and purification spells. Peppermint is good as a decongestant,

to clear the head and make you think more quickly. Even though this is a stimulating plant, sniffing peppermint can help you sleep, so place a fresh sprig beneath your pillow to drop off happily and dream true.

Colours

• Blue, especially clear sky blue, will help your mind to function at its best, and to keep you cool, calm and collected. It will also uplift you – the deeper shades of blue can bring out your spiritual side.

• Yellow echoes the bright side of your personality.

• Shiny fabrics, sequins, etc. Sparkle is 'you', and anything that glitters with many colours serves to emphasize your versatility and lively nature.

Stimulating peppermint will help you think clearly.

Correspondences for Number 6

Six correspondences promote harmony and co-operation, fostering community spirit.

Top tips: lapis lazuli will enable your Six Destiny number to express at the highest level while quartz warms a Six soul.

Rose Quartz

stones, and place them together in your partnership corner.

• LAPIS LAZULI This will help to awaken your spiritual side. To call your soulmate to you, take a piece of unsmoothed lapis and use it to carve a heart shape in a rose-pink candle. Light the candle, place the stone close by and stare at the flame, visualizing your love coming to you. Lapis strengthens fidelity – swap pieces with your lover to stay together.

Crystals

• ROSE QUARTZ Gentle rose quartz will attract romance and open your heart to all those who deserve your help and caring. It will also keep you affectionate and tolerant, which will bring you contentment. Wear a heart-shaped piece of rose quartz to attract love. To sweeten your love life, place a heart-shaped piece of rose quartz in the far right corner of your bedroom (which, according to Feng Shui, is the partnership area; see pages 80–3). If you want to attract a partner, select two similar pieces of rose quartz tumble-

Flowers

• ROSE This is the flower most linked with love, and it harmonizes with your nature. Sprinkle rose petals around the house for domestic bliss. A tea made of rosebuds, drunk before bedtime, will stimulate dreams of the future. Add rose petals to your bath, to make you gorgeous.

• COWSLIP The magic of spring appears in dainty cowslips. Their scent carries the mystery of the earth, and has healing properties. Carry cowslip to preserve youth, and place a cowslip beneath your doormat to discourage unwanted visitors.

Herbs, trees, oils and resins

- THYME Wearing a sprig of thyme in your hair is believed to make you irresistible. Thyme can also enable you to see fairies. Smell it to give you courage and increase your energy. Burn it to cleanse your home of all negativity.
- VANILLA Carry a vanilla bean to restore your vitality and focus your mind. The scent and taste of vanilla stimulate lust. Place a vanilla bean in your sugar bowl to create a loving atmosphere.

Colours

- Rose pink is warm, yet soothing. When worn, it will bring out the positive, tender aspects of your personality and will draw people to you.
- Soft blue has a calming effect and will enable you to maintain your serenity and balance.
- Coordinated colours, pastels and subtle blends and patterns are suited to your sensitive and discerning nature.

Rosebud tea can be sweet in many ways .

Correspondences for Number 7

Number Seven substances help you see beyond appearances and stimulate your sixth sense.
Top tips: carry beryl to follow a Seven life path when the going is tough. Sniff myrrh to make the best of a Seven Here-and-Now.

Crystals

• CLEAR QUARTZ If you carry a pointed piece of clear quartz it will boost your psychic powers. Placed beneath your pillow it encourages revealing dreams. To improve your well-being, place a quartz crystal in a clear glass containing fresh spring water, leave the glass in full sunshine for a day, remove the stone and drink the water.

• BERYL This was the original stone used for crystal balls. If you want to try this, hold your piece of beryl in a white cloth, look deep within it, let your mind go drowsy and see what reveals itself. Wear beryl to retain information. If you feel lethargic,

hold a piece of beryl in your hand and let its gentle, yet strong, energies empower you. If you have lost something, hold the beryl and visualize the missing object. Your intuition should then show you where it is.

Flowers

• POPPY These bright but ephemeral flowers remind us to 'seize the day'. The poppy is also associated with escape from this world, through drugs such as opium. Poppy seeds are used in mixtures to induce sleep. To find the answer to a question, write it on white paper and place this inside a poppy-seed pod. Slip it underneath your pillow and you will wake up with the answer.

• LOTUS In the east, the lotus has long been respected as a mystical symbol of life and the essence of the Universe. Carrying or wearing any segment of this flower attracts the blessings of the Gods.

Clear Quartz cluster

The pattern of the lotus petals can awaken the mystic within you.

Herbs, trees, oils and resins

• MYRRH Diffuse myrrh in an oil burner for peace and purity. It is an aid to meditation – add frankincense for a rich fragrance.

• EUCALYPTUS This is healing and confers protection. To enhance health, surround a green candle with eucalyptus leaves, and while the candle is burning visualize yourself, or the person you wish to heal, as totally robust (*not* 'getting better').

Colours

• Deep blue, deep purple and black enhance your dignity and mystery.

• Shades of lilac and pure white echo your spirituality.

• Unusual or daring colour combinations suit your radical and inventive streak, and flashes of flame red bring a message of renewal.

Correspondences for Number 8

Number eight substances promote success and power. Carry bloodstone to add oomph to your Eight personality and if Eight is your Destiny maximize your luck with ivy in your home and garden.

Onyx

Crystals

• BLOODSTONE This was carried in ancient Babylon to defeat enemies, and you can use it for the same purpose today. It will give you the courage to meet all challenges you face, and can enable you to follow the saying 'Don't get mad, get even!' Bloodstone also helps to attract wealth.

• ONYX This stone can protect you and your loved ones and give you strength. It can also focus your intuition and make you master of your destiny. Onyx will also help you when you need to keep things to yourself. If you need some extra psychic protection, light a black candle in front of a mirror. Place eight onyx tumble-stones

in a semicircle round the candle, on the side away from the mirror, and place a ninth stone 8cm (3in) to the right. Visualize any negative energy being channelled through the ninth stone, into the candle flame and from there through the mirror. The glass forms an entrance to the spirit dimension – anything negative being directed at you will now return to its sender. When your visualization is complete, blow out the flame, gather up your stones and cleanse them by leaving them overnight in a bowl of organic rice.

Flowers

• MARIGOLD Add this bright flower to your bathwater to win the respect of all you meet. Carry it in your pocket if you have to go to court and justice will smile on you.

• SNAPDRAGON Any part of snapdragon worn on your body will prevent people from deceiving you. Snapdragons can be used in the same way as onyx tumble-stones, to send anything negative back to the sender.

Nature is a peaceful reminder to keep your perspectives sensible.

Herbs, trees, oils and resins

• IVY This will bring you good luck if you carry it with you, or grow it around your house. It also repels any negativity, keeps disaster at bay and ensures that lovers remain faithful.

• COMFREY This herb has a reputation for keeping you and your possessions safe while you travel – pop a few leaves in your suitcase. It is even better if you have grown it in your garden, because it connects you with home. Comfrey root brings luck with money.

Colours

• Gold imparts an air of affluence and positivity and it can keep you cheerful when things get on top of you.

• Beige, grey, caramel and other fairly neutral colours are compatible with your air of authority and maturity.

• Dark and/or muted colours that are accented with expensive jewellery will create an impression of impeccable taste and success.

Correspondences for Number 9

Number nine correspondences encourage idealism and higher consciousness.

Top tips: labradorite earrings can keep your nine personality attuned to the highest vibrations and a nine soul soars with the scent of frankincense.

Crystals

• AMETHYST This spiritual stone will facilitate your reflective qualities and help your wisdom to grow. Placed by your bed it can give prophetic dreams. It is a wonderful companion during meditation. Wear it to help your concentration and keep you focused on your important goals in life. It can also ward off guilt and self-deception. This is a stone of peace – wear

Amethyst geode

an amethyst, so it touches your skin, to avoid becoming stressed. It can raise your spirits, ward off fears and focus you on a wider reality. It is a potent amulet while travelling.

• LABRADORITE This is a mystical stone that can raise your consciousness and also provide psychic protection if you have many people draining your energy. It will strengthen your faith in yourself and help ease you through change. Worn as a pendant it will encourage positive emotions and enable you to empathize without being compromised.

Flowers

• Bright golden MARIGOLD will help you to win the respect of everyone you meet if you float a few flowerheads in your bathwater. Marigolds plucked when the sun is at its height are said to strengthen the heart. A garland of marigolds strung around your door will keep anyone who wishes you harm at bay.

• IRIS has been used to purify the home since the time of the Romans – place the

fresh flowers in the room you want to revitalize. The flower has three points, which symbolize faith, wisdom and courage. Light a purple candle near your iris plant to stimulate these.

Herbs, trees, oils and resins

• FRANKINCENSE Used as an essential oil, this majestic fragrance is wonderful for meditation. It drives out all negativity and uplifts the soul. It can help you with your spiritual growth. Burn as a joss stick to raise the vibration of an area.

• NUTMEG This can be carried as a good luck charm. Sprinkle ground nutmeg on a green candle and light it, to attract money.

Colours

• Opulent purple will help you create an impression of gravitas and spirituality.

• Deep red resonates with your passion and involvement with life.

• Flamboyant colours, ethnic designs and adventurous contrasts can make a statement about your individuality.

Nutmeg has more than culinary uses. It can help you on your quests.

5: More Important Numbers

In addition to the five main numbers you are working with in life, there are other numbers that influence you. When you have become used to seeing how the Five Formulas operate, it will be interesting to look at how these other numbers can refine your understanding. Sometimes you will find that a number repeats, which will intensify its importance for you, or you may find that a number is largely, or completely, absent – this also will be significant.

Missing Numbers

To find out if you are missing a number, look at your entire birthdate and all the digits that appear in your name. If you were born in the 1900s, then you will not lack either 1 or 9, although these numbers appear in the birthdate of everyone born during the 20th century; if they are your *only* examples of 1 and 9, however, then these numbers may be relatively lacking.

Here is an example:

DANIEL JOHN MORRIS

14.7.1980

415953 1685 469991

Daniel's Destiny Number is Four, his Soul and Here-and-Now Numbers are both Nine, his Life Path Number is Three and his Personality Number is Five.

Nine is a particularly important number for Daniel, appearing as two of his Five Formulas and four times as a digit in his name. What is totally missing (from his birthdate and his name represented as numbers, as well as his Five Formulas) is Two, and that will prove to be significant in his life.

Missing numbers indicate experiences you may avoid, maybe because of what has happened to you in previous lifetimes or, if you do not believe in reincarnation, this missing number is simply a challenge for you, something with which you have to grapple. You may find that people in whom your missing number is strong annoy or irritate you. However, if you find your friends have a lot of your missing number – especially as Personality or Here-and-Now Numbers – then you are seeking what you lack, and that is very healthy.

Missing 1

Stand up for yourself. You may be afraid of speaking out, of taking the lead and being in any way unique or conspicuous. This could mean that you stay holed up in the back room, stifling your creativity and rarely being in any way original. Alpha personalities may frighten or overwhelm you, or you may resent them and become sullen and uncooperative around them.

You need to learn to take the lead – start by working out what your ambitions are and follow them without telling anyone. Make some new beginnings, and realize that you have a right to be *you*. Insist on what you know is right for you. While you may never be a great leader or innovator,

Once you start to be assertive you will find it gets easier with practice.

you can certainly learn to express yourself. If you find that many of your friends have a lot of One in their make-up, then you are coping well with your lack. No doubt you are learning from them how to be assertive. Supporting and advising may be a good role for you to fall into, but always make sure you do not lose sight of your individuality.

Missing 2

Tactless and impatient, you may lurch from one gaffe to another, leaving a trail of upset souls in your wake. The 'small print' passes you by – until it suddenly tangles you up so that you don't attend to more important things until it is too late. When you need help, there rarely seems to be anyone to give support. You need to become more aware of your behaviour and how it affects other people. It is not that you mean to be unkind, it is just that some things never occur to you – and you can change this with a bit of thought. Get into the habit of counting to 10, looking before you leap and really focusing on how what you say is affecting others. If you find that lots of your friends have a strong Two, then you are subconsciously increasing your empathy, and clearly you are not upsetting their delicate sensibilities. Ask them how they feel, and really listen to their answers.

Missing 3

Smile. Life does not have to be so serious. By being negative you can attract negativity, and it may seem that when you try to 'party' it feels forced, and you end up saying or doing the wrong thing and feeling like a wet blanket. You may long to be creative but find that spontaneity eludes you; while you may master the technique, there is little spark. You will have to learn to sell yourself, to let it all hang out and have a giggle. Seek out things that will make you laugh – humour is not a waste of time and play is the way we learn and grow, as every child knows. Look for the little child within you – it may help to try to recall the things you loved to do when you were small and help you to just mess about. There is originality within you, so relax and liberate it. If you find that you spend time with lots of Threes, then this is evidence that you are trying to channel that inner fun-lover and are sure to be enjoying life, even if you sometimes scare yourself by your self-indulgence and superficiality.

Reflecting on your problems can make them worse – better to get out there and do something.

Relax! Tension is a barrier to all that is worthwhile in life.

Missing 4

You cannot escape from the basics of life that we all have to struggle with, such as wet days, Mondays, bills, overdrafts and blocked sinks, so just roll up your sleeves and get on with it. Sometimes your recklessness causes you to be accident-prone and your lack of practicality gets you in a mess. If possible, you avoid hard work, and despite all the bright ideas in the world your lack of planning means that all too often things come to nothing. You need to discipline yourself and understand that grappling with life's basics will actually bring you a kind of freedom. Don't take shortcuts. Inevitably you will be faced with challenges, so discharge your obligations and you will find more outlets for your resourcefulness than you expected. If you have many friends who are strongly Four, then you are earnestly trying to develop their virtues, even if you are driving them crazy while you are doing it. Keep trying to be on time, complete with spare cash and umbrella, and pat yourself on the back for all the sensible things you achieve.

Missing 5

There is only one thing you can be sure of in life and that is change, so you had better get used to it. The best-laid plans can be blown apart by chance, and your comfort zone is not a safe place to hide. You tend to fear the new and untried. Discovery and adventure leave you cold, sex may seem dodgy and anything unpredictable gets strangled at birth. True experience of life is what you need, so you can embrace your humanity and be excited by things. It may seem that you often come up against emergencies – it is as if the Cosmos is telling you to expect the unexpected. Learn to ride the storm and be curious about what is around the corner. Uncover hidden aspects of yourself and welcome unpredictable and volatile people into your orbit. If they are there already then you are doing well, and learning to cope when everything goes crazy – you may even like it sometimes.

Missing 6

The sooner you really grow up and take responsibility for your actions, the sooner you will become aware of the love that surrounds you. Probably this escapes you. 'You choose your friends, not your family' you may mutter, but quite possibly you avoid the obligations of friendship, as well as resenting the demands of parents, partners, kids and domesticity. Home-making may be a chore, Christmas and birthdays a dread and having people

expect things of you a nuisance. When you realize the truth of 'it is more blessed to give than to receive', you will be on the road to balance. People will make what feel like unreasonable demands on you until you start to enjoy being needed and to appreciate and create beauty and harmony. If you are associated with lots of Sixes, then you are more mellow, and your heart is opening to love. The more you give, the more you will get.

Missing 7

Don't worry – it may never happen, unless your negative thinking is so indestructible that you create it. You often expect the worst and see portents of doom at every corner. Sometimes you are right, but your intuition is picking up the bad things while the good things escape. You probably believe that life is full of trouble and all that awaits us after death is oblivion. Possibly you will have to cope with setbacks and bad luck, until you start to have some faith in yourself and use your imagination creatively. Events will keep prodding you, until you discover a sense of meaning and realize that there is more to life than meets the eye. Open yourself to the possibility of the Unseen –

It's possible to retrain your mind – make a determined effort to count your blessings.

other worlds, other dimensions. Realize we do not know it all. Develop a sense of wonder. If you are surrounded by 'zoned-out', 'born-again' Seven hippies, that's great. You are realizing you are 'stardust'.

Missing 8

Life is tough, only the strong survive, and you don't feel like one of them. Financial decisions are a struggle, and when it comes to anything to do with business you don't have much of a clue. You may have many resources, but you find it hard to apply them. What you have achieved may feel dry, and you may be cheated of fulfilment, maybe through ill health or unsatisfactory relationships. Real success will cease to elude you when you stop being afraid of your own power and take control. Focus your abilities and give up being a soft touch. If you are offered a position of authority, take it. Apply for promotions, push yourself forward, meet challenges, confront unpleasant situations. You may not always win, but you will learn, and winning will eventually become more habitual. If you have many Eight associates, then you are finding out what it means to be effectual and that you can be a force to be reckoned with.

Missing 9

There is more to life than what is happening down your street, so isn't

it time you opened your mind and looked up at the stars? All you want is a quiet life and a peaceful one, proceeding from birth to death in an orderly fashion, but somehow you keep finding yourself in scary situations where people need your help. From 'tissue dramas' to car crashes, from heartbreak to heart attack – human beings seem to fall apart on your doorstep, and it is just what you *hate*. But there is a big, wide world out there and you need to become involved in it. The sooner you willingly take part, the sooner you will

find satisfaction from helping, instead of rising panic. We cannot control misfortune and suffering, but lending a hand makes it feel much better. However, if you have plenty of Nines around you, you are probably already helping others in some way, and learning to love doing it.

No missing numbers

If all of the numbers are represented in your make-up, this gives you balance and a full range of experience. You can probably understand and enter into most

Sometimes the most important thing in life is to ask the right question.

perspectives, and in life you may do a bit of everything, and be no stranger to any emotion. This is a good thing but can also lead to you being bored sometimes. Look to the number(s) that you have least of, and see if you can experience something new or develop a little more in that area. Never become complacent – there is always another challenge, another level to rise to.

The Higher Numbers

The most important numbers are those from 1 to 9, to which all the others reduce. However, there are nuances of meaning attached to the Higher Numbers, and these will be present in you if the digits within your birthdate, or in your name, add up to them in the first instance before reducing to a single figure. These Higher Numbers are particularly important if they are your birthday. They carry within them the influence of their component digits as well as the final sum. Eleven and Twenty-Two are Master Numbers, and are dealt with in their own section – see pages 206–11.

TEN: Your vitality and determination is enhanced by wisdom and a subtle awareness, but you can be very stubborn. Your creativity is especially potent.

TWELVE: You have an intense need to express yourself which you do dynamically but also with empathy for others, which makes you effectual, even though you can be a tad picky at times!

THIRTEEN: This does not have to be an unlucky number, but spiritual awareness needs to be blended with responsibility and creativity used realistically – then you can move mountains!

FOURTEEN: You want to make things happen and you have a story to tell. However, you may get tangled up in your thoughts. You need a focus, and clarity.

FIFTEEN: Sensual and loving, you can sometimes be carried away by your own desires. If you listen to what others say, you will find greatest fulfilment.

SIXTEEN: Introspective and questioning, you want both closeness and independence. Learn to trust your intuition and go with the flow.

SEVENTEEN: You are very strong-willed and are aware of the workings of Fate in your life. Determined to achieve, you are also attuned to deeper meanings.

EIGHTEEN Aware of the needs and feelings of others, you can be pragmatic and decisive about getting results. Try to avoid power struggles and making judgements.

Thirteen can be a powerful number if you have courage.

30 somethings – party animals !

NINETEEN: You are zealous and inspired and when you see the right way you want to enthuse others. You need to watch out for a self-righteous streak, but you are ambitious and far-sighted.

TWENTY: Fairness motivates you and partnerships are vital. You have strong feelings but also doubts can plague you, leaving you moody.

TWENTY-ONE: Creative and happy-go-lucky, you want to cheer up the world. You want both to lead and cooperate and may fall between two stools, but you revel in abundance.

TWENTY-THREE: Life is an adventure and your sensuality is strong. You attract people with your lively charm but sometimes you go off on an adventure in a world of your own.

TWENTY-FOUR: Looking after the creature comforts of others is key, and you are a true home-builder. Just be aware that you can't be responsible for everything.

TWENTY-FIVE: Adventurous and intuitive, you may blow hot and cold as feelings alternate with analysis. Respect your gut instincts and communicate.

TWENTY-SIX: Charismatic and also supportive, you can go far by attuning to the needs of others. Your need to be needed must not become a power trip.

TWENTY-SEVEN: Honest and empathic, you may feel buffeted by the realities of life. Sometimes there are no rights and wrongs. If you think positively you can do wonders.

TWENTY-EIGHT: Strong-willed and creative, you have energy, drive and flair, but you can also be pushy, so give other people their space.

TWENTY-NINE: Your emotions are larger-than-life and you can be tempestuous, although you seek justice. It is important not to expect too much of life and partners.

THIRTY: A real party animal, you gravitate towards the bright lights. Although you may seem self-expressive and extrovert, sometimes you do wonder what it all means.

THIRTY-ONE: You may have masses of staying-power and can apply your imagination practically and dynamically, but you can be pessimistic at times.

Consonants: Your Quiescent Self

The consonants in your name show where and how the flow of sound as the names are enunciated, is interrupted. The sum of the consonants adds up to your quiescent self – the 'you' that exists when you are totally relaxed and alone. This 'you' tends to disappear as soon as anyone else enters your space. Your quiescent self emerges in dreams and fantasies, and may show itself in body language and physical characteristics. It may disappear as soon as conversation starts. It has a mystery about it, and is your secret, but it may also be partly or completely concealed from you. Think about your quiescent self. You may be busy expressing your more dominant characteristics and missing this essential clue.

Number 1 quiescent self

Deep inside you want to be a pioneer with others admiring you for your chutzpah and derring-do. You long to excel. Actually you may appear more forceful, stronger and self-centred than you realize.

Number 2 quiescent self

You long to be loved and protected and you dream of having people to care for, in a peaceful place. You may give the initial impression of being shy, gentle and sweet.

Number 3 quiescent self

A little lime-light would be lovely. You fantasize about being everyone's favourite – attractive and talented. Initially you appear bubbly, extrovert and friendly.

Number 4 quiescent self

You want to be loyal, dependable and honest, so that everyone trusts you and sees you as efficient. You probably seem to have plenty of stamina and dignity.

Number 5 quiescent self

The wild gypsy, the free spirit, secretly you would love to have no ties and to travel widely. You may have lots of sexual fantasies. Instinctively you appear sexy and freedom loving.

Number 6 quiescent self

In your heart of hearts you would like to be a mystic, a scientist or a priest, left alone to reflect. You give the impression of being very private, refined and remote.

Number 5 – these are free spirited souls.

Number 7 quiescent self
In your heart of hearts you would like to be a mystic, a scientist or a priest, left alone to reflect. You give the impression of being private, refined and a bit distant.

Number 8 quiescent self
You dream of power, wealth and success and come across more confident than you realise – people may think you have reached the top when you are far from it!

Number 9 quiescent self
You would love to serve humanity and you see yourself as a celebrated artist, leader or lover. You come across as empathic, passionate and flamboyant.

6: Relationships

Relationships with other people are the most important elements in the lives of the majority of us. Numerology can enable us to understand each other.

Numerological Relationships

Relationships exist on many levels. As individuals we are complex enough, and this is doubled when we couple up with another person. Your numerological profile will influence what you expect from and give to any relationship, and will also determine your ideas about relationships themselves. Different types of relationships will evoke different aspects of your personality. Numerology does not determine whether a relationship will, or will not, work out. What it can do is give you an idea of the easy and difficult elements, and show you what you are dealing with.

In comparing your numerological profile with another person, start by setting out your Five Formulas in order, vertically, starting with your Personality Number, then your Life Path Number, followed by Soul, Destiny and Here-and-Now Numbers. List your partner's equivalent numbers alongside, so you can compare them directly (see opposite). You will then be able to see how you interact. If you have several numbers that are the same – for instance, if you both have a Personality of One, a Life Path of Eight and a Soul Number of Two – then you will be very similar in many respects. This can be either a good thing or a challenge.

For example, if you share a One Personality, you will understand each other's need for independence, but could both end up doing your own thing or becoming irritable with the other if they get in your way. A similar Life Path Number means you are both on the same track, with similar values. This is good for business, but it could mean you encourage each other to ignore other choices. A shared Soul Number is a good indication for romantic relationships, but a possible disadvantage is that expectations may be high, and when things go wrong (maybe because other numbers in your profile are less compatible) deep disappointment could set in. Shared Destiny Numbers can bind you closely but not necessarily comfortably, and a shared Here-and-Now Number could result in competition, although it is dynamic for friends.

Perhaps the most encouraging result for important relationships is to find the same

COMPARISON CHARTS

Here is an example of how to set out the five formulas of two people, for comparison. You can use the space on pages 388–91 to write out your own formulas.

	JAKE HUNT 1+1+2+5+8+3+5+2	ANNA MARKS 1+5+5+1+4+1+9+2+1
PERSONALITY	3	8
LIFE PATH	3.7.1982 = 3	8.3.1985 = 7
SOUL	9	3
DESTINY	9	2
HERE-AND-NOW	9	3

numbers but in different places. If your Life Path Number is a Seven and your partner's Soul Number is Seven, then he or she can give you inspiration that will help you on your way without being suffocating. Similar numbers in differing places can be stimulating, giving interesting interconnections within the partnership. However, in the end the choice is yours and with awareness you can make it work if the will is there on both sides.

Number 1

At first glance it may seem that relationships are not very important to this number, but if One is strong in your make-up you will know that is not the case at all. One has a yearning to find that special someone, and may be very idealistic about it. Some Ones have a fixed image about the kind of partner they want and may search for a lifetime, possibly enduring many disappointments, without giving up. Ones may enthusiastically repeat the same mistakes time after time, as they chase an enduring dream that gives them ceaseless inspiration.

Some do choose a solitary path, sooner or later, and, while it is true that Ones are happier on their own than many other numbers, the fact that One is strong in your character does not doom you to a life as a 'sad, strange little person' – far from it. You can be a very dedicated person, with a great deal to give another party. Sometimes you can be devoted to the interests and well-being of another, even to your own detriment. However, there is generally something unilateral in your approach and you have to be careful that your counterpart does not feel like one of your 'projects'. It can be hard for you really to see another person – they may appear through the lens of your own beliefs. While you are the last person to want to restrict the choices of anyone, sometimes your approach can *feel* restricting, as your partner struggles to be seen by you.

Tips

- Each party must retain a strong measure of independence
- Sharing of actual tasks and activities should be limited – things will work better if each has their own area to look after
- Remember that even without realizing it you may make assumptions, or start doing something on your own – keep telling yourself to discuss and communicate
- Good relationships are created by hard work rather than chemistry or love at first sight and, if you remember that, you will succeed

DOMINANT 1'S COMPATIBILITY

John is Anna's boss. With 1 as his Personality and Life Path he is very driven. Anna's 8 personality resonates to his ambition while their shared 3 Soul indicates they will feel at ease with each other and may share jokes and fun times. However Anna's 7 Life Path suggests she may need a job with a meaningful spiritual purpose. John totally lacks 7 and may not be able to satisfy this.

	JOHN AMOS 1+6+8+5+1+4+6+1	ANNA MARKS 1+5+5+1+4+1+9+2+1
PERSONALITY	1	8
LIFE PATH	1.9.1962 = 1	8.3.1985 = 7
SOUL	3	3
DESTINY	5	2
HERE-AND-NOW	2	3

If you can only remember a few basics, you can have brilliant relationships, partly because there is a limit to what you expect personally from your partner. True respect, support, companionship with independence – all these are well within your reach if you remember that you and your 'significant other' are like twin pillars of a temple, standing side by side, yet separate.

As a lover and a life partner

You may be passionate and devoted. If you decide a person is 'the one', you may pursue them for years. This may be especially true if One is your Soul Number. With One as a Life Path or Personality Number, you may be especially idealistic about the relationship and hate the thought of splitting up – this may seem like a failure. If One is your Here-and-Now Number, you like to feel that you have bagged the best 'catch' – don't let your competitiveness blind you to core values. If One is your Destiny Number, you may wish your partner to add to your status. All of these purposes are fine – relationships are complex matters and not just about wine and roses. However, they need to be paired with true emotion. You know this very well, but you may charge off down the road to commitment before you realize that you have made the wrong choice. Always make sure that you have an escape clause, for the sake of the other party as much as yourself, and try not to expect the world. Relationships are what you make them. Having said this, avoid being obsessed about keeping a bad relationship going – if it is time to get out, pack your bags.

As a friend

Loyal and devoted, you throw a great deal into your friendships and may be very excited when you think you have found someone who feels, thinks and acts like you. You can be friends for life, but your best bet is not to get *too* close, or the differences between you may become more apparent than is comfortable. Be clear what you want from a friend – no one is going to be on your side all the time, and you should not have to champion anyone else through thick and thin. The spaces in your friendships will help them endure as much as the closeness will.

As a business partner

This is an area that requires a lot of thought. If One is strong in your make-up, especially as Personality or Life Path Number, working with another person may be difficult, if not impossible. If you are going to set up in partnership with someone, you need to be sure that you have total autonomy in your sphere of action, that you really can trust the other person completely to do what he or she promises, and that, even if you are not technically the boss, no one else is bossing you. Given the right conditions, you can work well with others, but if things go wrong they will go very, very wrong – so be warned.

Often when we shout loudest, we are listened to least.

Number one is by no
means as solitary a soul
as some might assume.

COMPATIBILITY

With 1   Works really well. If you each pursue a parallel course, you will appear to be the happiest couple around.

With 2   This can be very creative and fun as long as Two has other people to cosy up with, or you could find it cloying. Value and celebrate your differences.

With 3   Your dynamism and Three's cheerful resourcefulness can be very effectual in a practical way, as long as you don't get bogged down with the inconvenient practicalities.

With 4   The down-to-earth approach of Four can mean that you achieve fabulous things. However, you need to be careful that you don't end up arguing, as you could see Four as trying to frustrate you or tie you up in red tape. They are only trying to make your plans workable.

With 5   Together you can create beautiful things and situations, and your partnership can benefit the community. However, you are both volatile – you must stop, think and count to 10. Communication is key.

With 6   Your partnership will lead you both to question life deeply and maybe to learn from your association. You may feel that fate is at work, and if that thought inspires you it can transform you and take your relationship to soul level.

With 7   You operate on different levels. With mutual respect you can build something enduring, or end up in a power struggle – don't go there.

With 8   You both want to be boss but as long as you negotiate your area of independence and let Eight work on general structure, this can work to make a life of change and adventure.

With 9   Make or break. You have to have shared purposes and if this is cemented you are going places. This is where you will most need to compromise – but it could be worth it.

Number 2

Relationships are absolutely central to you, and you may not feel complete
without them. With Two as your Soul Number, you may yearn deeply for
that special person to make your life complete, and this may be always in
the back of your mind. With Two as your Personality Number, you probably
always have someone good-looking at your side. With Two as your Life Path
Number, a long-term partnership is probably one of your main ambitions in
life. With Two as your Destiny Number, you may feel it is almost your duty to
make a good partnership, and feel guilty if you cannot do this.

STRONG 2

Ellen is Anna's mother. Her numerology make-up is strongly 2. Anna shares this in
her Destiny Number, suggesting she may feel her mother is instrumental at shaping
the way her life works out. Ellen may feel threatened by Anna's ambitious 8 and
secretive 7 but their shared 3 shows they'll find much to enjoy together.

	ELLEN MARKS 5+3+3+5+5+4+1+9+2+1	ANNA MARKS 1+5+5+1+4+1+9+2+1
PERSONALITY	2	8
LIFE PATH	2.9.1953 = 2	8.3.1985 = 7
SOUL	11/2	3
DESTINY	2	2
HERE-AND-NOW	3	3

You have a huge amount to bring to any partnership, and often you feel deeply shaken and mystified when you split up. You give so much, try so hard – what more could you have done? The problem is that you may do *too* much, and this can be overwhelming for the other party. Sometimes your partner may feel that when they look at you they are seeing a reflection of themselves, and this may be uncomfortable and frustrating. To make your partnerships work you need to have a 'relationship' with something other than your partner. This could be a hobby or a vocation, it might be art or music, but it needs to be something that is yours alone. Through this sort of passion your lover can come to see and value the real you in all your vibrancy.

However, Two can also be the number of conflict, and occasionally you may pick a fight and be critical and complaining. The deeper drive that is at work when this happens is the wish to face and iron out difficulties, in search of the perfect union. Unsurprisingly, this rarely works, and differences are more likely to become polarized. Then you may go into a huge sulk – Two can bring an ongoing feud at its worst. It is best to work at seeing the positive and also at being realistic, because not everything has to always be sweetness and light to make it a good partnership.

Two loves to be in a relationship but it isn't always plain sailing.

Tips

- Take off the rose-tinted spectacles – real life and real people can be good enough
- Don't take things too much to heart – a person can think you are imperfect and still love you very much
- If you are dissatisfied, comment on the *behaviour*, not the person
- If you are hurt, say how you feel and avoid being judgemental

As a lover and a life partner

Nothing is too much trouble and you are devoted to the creature comforts of your lover. Organizing and cleaning, shopping and cooking, you may see your role as that of the supportive one, while your partner goes out to conquer the world. This can work well when there is a division of labour that both parties are satisfied with – and that both honour. Sometimes, however, you can be let down when your lover does not keep up their end of the bargain. It is possible that you may assume your partner is fulfilling a role when in fact they have not made that agreement at all. It is very important that you communicate your wishes and feelings because your lover may not be able to read your mind. Be careful also that you don't become a 'doormat', because then you will be walked on. You need lots of security, reassurance and kisses and cuddles and you are a 'natural' at creating a peaceful and loving environment. Just remember to give your loved one their own space, and they will always come back to you.

The image of a happy couple tugs at the heart of almost every person.

As a friend

You love to have a 'best mate' and you can be a bit jealous if anyone else tries to get too close. If your friend has a problem, you will drop everything to be with them. The only problem is that you may smother your friends and then wonder why they pull away. You may also be a little over-dependent on the views and approval of your friends, so practise saying no sometimes. However, you are always sympathetic, always soothing, always helpful – who could ask for more?

As a business partner

You make a great business partner if you can take on a secondary role, organizing the administration, chatting to customers, making tea and smiling. Your associate should make the decisions, provide the impetus and 'slay the dragons'. For someone who is prepared to do this, you are an angel to have at their side. From your point of view, you need to be sure that you can trust your counterpart – check out the 'small print' and don't expect to be looked after, because that might not happen. It is also important for you to take your emotions out of the working environment as much as you can – you are in this for profit. Look elsewhere for the warm cuddle.

COMPATIBILITY

With 1   This can be very exciting with lots of thrills, spills and giggles, but you could find that your feelings are trampled on, so you must fight your corner sensibly and not get over-emotional. If you each fall into role, it could dovetail brilliantly.

With 2   This could be heaven or hell, as you both need so much and you can both be touchy. Feelings will run high, and you must discuss things before it gets out of hand. Sulks are banned. Create something of practical value and use together.

With 3   There could be spats – it is important that you don't mistake the playfulness of Three for lack of caring. Make sure you have lots to do, places to go and people to see.

With 4   You will love to play happy Families and everyone is welcome at your house. You have the beautiful ideas and Four makes them work. Make sure you don't get bored.

With 5   You will find you are looking deeply into yourself and the relationship will make you a wiser person. A mysterious chemistry could keep you coming back for more, but this is not an easy ride.

With 6   You could get fixated on status symbols and keeping up with the neighbours. However, you should have a beautiful home and feel that you are really getting somewhere as a couple.

With 7   You each have something to teach the other because your outlooks are very different, but together you will travel mentally and physically. An intriguing parternship.

With 8   It may seem as if you are connecting, but empathy may be elusive. You each need to have your own space and neither must try too hard to control things. Mutual respect works wonders.

With 9   Although you are very different people, you may feel that you have what you want, keeping the home fires burning until Nine swans in. Make sure you listen to what your partner wants and things could work well.

Finding your soul mate is the dream of Two.

Number 3

Bubbly, light-hearted and friendly, it is easy for you to enter into relationships of all kinds. You get invited to parties while waiting in the supermarket queue and find romance at the bus stop. But it may be 'easy come, easy go', for you can be quickly bored. First impressions count with you, and you can be a sucker for charm, audacity and the 'drop dead' gorgeous. But sooner or later you find out that handsome is as handsome does, and you may be disappointed to realize that below the surface things are not so great. Not that you are prone to dig and delve; often you prefer to stay with the superficial. This goes for your own emotions too – solemn vows are not your style.

Tips

- The couple that plays together, stays together
- Whatever partnership you settle into, make sure there will be plenty of variety in your life
- Don't judge a book by the cover – the most gripping stuff often comes in a plain wrapper
- Changing partners can bring 'same old, same old' – sometimes it is more fun to pep up an existing relationship

With Three as your Personality Number, you probably crackle with confidence. It is easy for you to attract people, but you may try too hard to impress them at first – remember that you don't have to be the centre of attention all the time in order to be liked and successful. With Three as your Life Path Number, you may well have an entourage of people who want to be your friend or lover and it may be hard for you to settle with individuals. Like it or not, in the end you will need to think deeply about whom you spend time with, if you want to avoid feeling discontented. With Three as your Destiny Number, you may feel it is up to you to entertain people. You may also fear being tied down and having your wings clipped. It will help if you can realize that the right partner can actually

STRONG 3 PERSONALITY

Karen is Anna's younger sister. She has a strongly 3 personality. Anna will probably feel relaxed and giggly around her because she stimulates her 3 Soul and Here-and-Now. Karen will find she can leave behind her sensible 4 image and express her bubbly Personality and pursue her creative Life Path and Destiny.

	KAREN MARKS 2+1+9+5+5+4+1+9+2+1	ANNA MARKS 1+5+5+1+4+1+9+2+1
PERSONALITY	3	8
LIFE PATH	3.9.1989 = 3	8.3.1985 = 7
SOUL	7	3
DESTINY	3	2
HERE-AND-NOW	4	3

make you feel *more* free, by bringing out your latent talents. If Three is your Soul Number, you find great joy in all associations. You will be generous about expressing your love and sexually uninhibited, but try to accept that not everyone can be so relaxed and giving.

Wherever the Number Three appears in your make-up, it will bring a touch of the flirty and the fickle. You may be 'touchy-feely' and sensual, but you hate to feel trapped, and Three can often bring the Eternal Triangle, where you are the 'other woman' or 'other man'. When this happens it is because you are avoiding commitment. You are reluctant to tie yourself to one life partner, but you can find fulfilment in permanent relationships where your freedom is respected and you can then be devotedly faithful.

As a lover and a life partner

Never a dull moment. If you are not chattering non-stop, you are dashing off on some new adventure. Partners may find it hard to keep up with you – they need to be good listeners who are stable and secure in themselves, or party animals like you. Whoever you are with, you have an eye for other attractive individuals. It is much better if this is not taken too seriously, because you will soon be distracted or change your mind. What appeals to you one day may bore you the next, and any association has to offer fun and a smorgasbord of experience. Just as everyone is about to give up on you as an incorrigible flirt, you take the plunge into a lasting relationship. It may be a mystery even to you what has happened, but at last the thought of breaking up seems a drag, not to mention sad and boring – and you are hooked.

As a friend

You are a brilliant companion for anyone who wants a good time, ready to hit the hot spots and have a laugh together. You are always there with a big hug and a grin but, although you have lots of things to give, exclusivity may not be one of them. The 'best mate' idea won't appeal

Laughter can bring a couple closer together.

if it limits you. You love to enjoy company without too much being expected of you. What you see is what you get – but it is amazing, so who is complaining?

As a business partner
'Success' is your middle name and you bring luck to any partnership as long as you are not tied into a nine-to-five treadmill. You are the one who talks the talk and spies the main chance and you need a partner who will provide the stability and the planning. If you are not over-casual, and if you don't stretch the expense account to breaking point, you are a gift to anyone who is ambitious.

The enterprise of Three needs to be kept on target by a partner.

COMPATIBILITY

With 1   Lots of solid achievement, as One keeps you on track and makes your talents count. If you get fed up with being bossed about, think of all the benefits and laugh it off.

With 2   'Snap, crackle, pop' – sensuous as lovers, but Two could cling and Three play around. Talk, don't argue. In business you can complement each other, with tolerance.

With 3   Together you are beautiful. You can make the world a better place or create a fabulous home as long as you don't compete.

With 4   Like it or not, you will have to think deeply about life. The structure of Four can help you be effectual and fulfilled, so work at it.

With 5   You can conquer the world or end up with horns locked. Keep approaching your goals from different angles and always have something inspiring to aim for, together.

With 6   This is a voyage of discovery for you both. Your partnership functions best if you are involved in the community, or travelling together.

With 7   People may be surprised at how two such dissimilar people can hit it off – but it may happen. Seven wakes your spiritual side and you may be inseparable and unstoppable.

With 8   You need to sort out routines and each have your area to concentrate on. This relationship works better if you can transcend selfish concerns. The 'power tripping' of Eight could enrage or excite you.

With 9   You will have a ball, and when the partying is over you will know whether there is anything deeper or it was just a fling. Either way it will be memorable.

Number 4

The person who coined the phrase 'familiarity breeds contempt' could not have had much Four in their make-up. The tried-and-tested pleases you, and love tends to grow rather than strike out of the blue. The way into your heart may be for the other party to become indispensable, through simply being there day to day, so you come to rely on their presence. Trust and reliability are essential to you, and you don't readily open your heart. When you do, however, you can be utterly faithful and committed. You will support your partner through thick and thin and, while your help may be practical rather than emotional, you show your love in everything you do.

With Four as your Personality Number, you will probably want to ask mutual friends all about the character of anyone you are contemplating getting close to. If Four is your Life Path or Destiny Number, you could well marry your childhood sweet-heart, or maybe find your way back together with them after a gap – with you the first cut is the deepest. If Four is your Soul Number, your loyalty is almost painful and you are really capable of 'till death do us part' – home-making is deeply important to you and you invest a lot in it. Four as your Here-and-Now Number can sometimes get you stuck with the wrong person, because you find it hard to make the break once your friends see you as an 'item'. You would hate to be seen as a love cheat, which is greatly to your credit but can get you bogged down.

Four appearing anywhere in your make-up adds a big dose of stability in all associations. You are comfortable with clear boundaries in any relationship, so that who does what can be relied on. You like to know where you stand, you say what you mean and mean what you say (although you do not always express everything you feel). Any relationship works much better for you when a mutual routine has been established, and you open out to your partner more and more as you see they are in the same place, doing the same things, in a regular manner. However, there is also an earthy playfulness about you, and a dry sense of humour.

Tips

- Make sure that the practicalities of any relationship are sorted out, fair and square, from the start. This means money needs to be discussed in detail. Avoid this at your peril
- Caution is one thing; fear is quite another. Sometimes, when taking the plunge, 'feel the fear and do it anyway' has to be your motto
- You may not value appearances, but others do, so maximize your chances by getting dressed up
- It may be hard to imagine why others get emotional or need excitement, but you need to accept this as a fact and deal with it sympathetically

As a lover and a life partner

Glamorous looks may not be high on your agenda, but you are nonetheless very sensual and sexy when you relax. However, you may get almost as big a thrill from a cuddle on the sofa as from sex. You reserve romantic gestures for special occasions and then you tend to follow the established pattern, such as red roses on Valentine's Day. Meeting the material needs of your partner and having your own met are both very important. 'When the wolf comes in at the door, loves creeps out of the window' is the kind of thing you might say. Love in a shack does not sound romantic to you – you want to be able to pay the mortgage. However, if you are committed you will work extremely hard to meet the bills. You can be passionate, but deep down friendship matters most to you, because you know it lasts.

As a friend

From menu-planning to house-moving, you are there with a helping hand – in fact you may get almost offended if you are not called upon. Your circle of friends is fairly stable, with new acquaintances added slowly; you like to stay in touch with the people you went to school with, and you love those reunions. You support the fabric of society almost single-handedly, and when anyone loses their address book you have always got a back-up of contacts to share. In an uncertain world, your friendship is a priceless gem.

As a business partner

You are a fabulous partner for anyone who wants someone reliable to back up the files, organize the records and always be there without fail to open the office. You will be happy for your partner to dazzle the world as long as they bring in the business. Chatting up and dashing about is not your style. Support a person who can do these things, and you are both laughing all the way to the bank.

Fours love to share material comforts with their partners.

A LIFE OF 4

Paul is Anna's father. The emphasis on 4 in his Life Path and Destiny have made him reliable and moderately successful. Anna's 8 Personality finds a secure base with him but her 7 Life Path may mean she feels he does not understand what she is about and sometimes she may find him short-sighted.

	PAUL MARKS 7+1+3+3+4+1+9+2+1	ANNA MARKS 1+5+5+1+4+1+9+2+1
PERSONALITY	8	8
LIFE PATH	8.1.1948 = 4	8.3.1985 = 7
SOUL	5	3
DESTINY	4	2
HERE-AND-NOW	5	3

COMPATIBILITY

With 1   This can be a sparkling and profitable association – you each have your own abilities. Keep those boundaries in place, but have lunch or a game of tennis together every so often.

With 2   Lovely domesticity – your home can be second to none. This could be very snug, but there could also be moods and atmospheres, so learn to talk.

With 3   Chalk and cheese, but there is a chemistry here that can flow for both of you, in marriage, business or friendship. You must work at being open-minded or at least accepting.

With 4   You could turn into ships that pass in the night, but neither of you may mind as long as it is the same ship, at the same time. If things dovetail, money and status should arrive.

With 5   This partnership will take you both on a journey. It is going to be uncomfortable at times, but you should have a sense of achievement and fulfilment.

With 6   You both have the same priorities and complement each other in a comfortable way. However, you need to be careful that you don't become joined at the hip.

With 7   You both sense something unattainable in the other that keeps you hooked. You may row but the making up will be blissful. Don't analyse – compromise.

With 8   You are going places materially and practically and the sex is probably wonderful. Sometimes you could feel out of your depth, but be confident. You are a co-creator here.

With 9   Learn to appreciate each other and one day you will be celebrating your diamond jubilee. Otherwise you could be stuck in a rut blaming each other. Take responsibility and build on what is good.

Four can aim high with an enterprising other half.

Number 5

With Five strong in your make-up, you will look to your relationships
to provide you with excitement, although you may get overwrought or
impatient if someone tries to mess you around. You are probably very
popular, but sometimes you let people down because you are trying to
keep too many balls in the air, or you just get distracted. However, your
unreliability can serve to make you more sought after – everyone knows
that when you are around the atmosphere tends to electrify.

You are avidly interested in people because
you realize that everyone has a story to
tell, and you may ask lots of questions.
Your intensity can be very flattering, but
sometimes you spoil things a little by
interrupting mid-sentence, or calling out
to someone else. It suits you to be the
centre of a buzzing crowd, and often you
will be listening to what the person behind
you is saying, while you are nodding and
smiling at your companion.

With Five as your Personality or Here-and-
Now Number, it is 'the more the merrier'

Tips

• Accept that to keep in any relationship you have to give some
commitment – to find that no one trusts you could be boring in
the long run
• Use your communicative skills to talk about your feelings and, if
you are not sure what they are, say that
• Avoid rationalizing your feelings
• Excitement and variety are essential – never try to do without
them, but always try to inject them into an existing relationship

278

Fives can bring
many changes in
partnerships, but
lasting love comes
with the right
person.

with just about all types of relationships. You may have a reputation for being flighty, which makes you smile and shrug – until you want someone to take you seriously. Then you may have to use all your powers of persuasion. If Five is your Life Path or Destiny Number, you may find it very hard to stick with one partner, friend or colleague, or you may maintain a very wide circle of friends – social networking websites are a godsend to contact-obsessed Five. With Five as your Soul Number, a 'meeting of true minds' is essential, and you long for someone who is on the same wavelength and with whom you can have understanding, along with stimulating conversations.

Five anywhere in your make-up can predispose you to lots of changes, unexpected encounters and maybe unusual liaisons. You will probably travel

STRONG 5 PERSONALITY

Sally is Jake's mother. Her lively and unpredictable Personality and Life Path 5 will have helped the creativity and playfulness of his 3. However, the 9 side of him may despair of his mum's butterfly nature and he may wonder why she does not support him wholeheartedly in his campaigns.

	SALLY HUNT 1+1+3+3+7+8+3+5+2	JAKE HUNT 1+1+2+5+8+3+5+2
PERSONALITY	5	3
LIFE PATH	5.2.1951 = 5	3.7.1982 = 3
SOUL	2	9
DESTINY	6	9
HERE-AND-NOW	6	9

about a lot in order to keep in contact, and may enjoy forming relationships with people from different cultures or backgrounds. In relationships, as in all things, you may ask 'why not?' and this can make for some interesting situations. Whatever the connection, communication is key – you need people who can click with you intellectually and provide you with alternative perspectives.

As a lover and a life partner

Your 'pulling shoes' are always polished and you are, it has to be said, an incorrigible flirt. 'Love 'em and leave 'em', 'a girl or guy in every port' – you are quite capable of serial one-night stands, two-timing and dumping by text. Your sex appeal crackles and your libido is strong, and you like your partner to keep you on a high. Yes, you are a bit anti-commitment, but you are also able to form a deep and meaningful relationship with someone with whom you have a mental connection. You might consider a *ménage à trois* or other unconventional set-up, and if you are true to yourself you don't meekly follow the traditional model. This means you can bring the kind of emotional honesty to a partnership that can seal it for a lifetime, with a bit of luck.

As a friend

You like someone you can have a discussion with, who is flexible and who really sparks you off, intellectually. It is also great to have a 'partner in crime', to accompany you on adventures. Lots of people think of you as their mate, and you are really easy to get along with. But deep inside it takes a lot for you truly to call a person 'friend', and that will be based on mental rapport and the merit that you place on their opinions. Your friends really value your detached, quirky perspective and the way you make them smile, however hard things seem – and if there is a way out you will find it.

As a business partner

You are probably the brains behind the organization, resourceful and well informed. You can sell anything to anyone, and you are a master net-worker. Probably you will be the one who organizes publicity, websites and similar. Restless, and with a low boredom threshold, you need a stable partner to hold the fort, keep to schedules and make the tea. Don't drive them crazy.

Fives find domestic bliss by welcoming variety and discussion.

COMPATIBILITY

With 1	Blissful and harmonious – you go your separate ways, but reunion is always stimulating, and it is great to feel you really are doing some good in the world.
With 2	It is really hard to get a grip on this relationship and Two could seem too clingy and needy, but there is still an attraction and you keep trying to analyse it.
With 3	You can set the world alight, but there could be power struggles as each of you may want the limelight. Money and property could come, but it could also go again without some restraint, so think about it.
With 4	You complement each other wonderfully, but you may both struggle to see this unless you make the effort to rise above your preconceptions. This relationship can make you both less selfish.
With 5	Lots of talk, but is anyone listening? You could both end up quite lonely, or you could find you are true soulmates, heading in the same direction.
With 6	A creative partnership, so don't let moods and pickiness get in the way. You may need to scale down your expectations until you sort out your differences.
With 7	You find each other fascinating and you can have some fabulous times together. You will need a project to work on if your relationship is going to be more than just sex and rock'n'roll.
With 8	Together you can move mountains and set down some solid foundations for life together, but the danger is you could feel trapped. Negotiate for more space.
With 9	You association is likely to be unconventional and lively. One minute you are in your element, the next you wonder if you are out of your depth. Keep talking.

Number 6

You find your greatest fulfilment in association with other people and you work hard at relationships of all types. A true romantic, love is always your goal, although your idealism can cause you to be let down. Never mind! Hope springs eternal and you are soon involved again. You are good at compromise, and put harmony above your own wishes, although you can be a little selfish at times when it comes to your creature comforts, security and the attractive possessions with which you surround yourself.

You prefer any partnership to fit into your circle of friends – not for you the 'gruesome twosome', 'you-and-me-against-the-world' scene. Creating something together, going out in a group, interacting with other couples – all of this is important to you in any relationship.

With Six as your Soul Number, you pour your heart and soul into your partnerships, and you may cry easily with joy or sorrow. Six as a Life Path or Destiny Number lifts relationships and family life almost to a vocation. With Six as your Personality or Here-and-Now Number, you will be very aware of how you appear as a couple – you will love to portray an image of perfection. Six anywhere in your make-up can make you competitive in relationships. When other people may moan about their partners or seek support in unpleasant domestic situations,

Tips

- Most people will want to relate to *you*, not to a cast of thousands in the shape of your friends and extended family, so don't ask too much of partners in this respect
- Don't bear a grudge – concentrate on something positive instead
- Limit jealousy by learning to love yourself and value your good qualities
- Work hard at keeping romance alive – don't expect it just to 'happen'

STRONG 6 PERSONALITY

Sam is Sally's husband. His very strong 6 emphasis indicates that he will love peace and a lovely home. He may find Sally's lively 5 unsettling at times, but her 6 Destiny shows family links and their shared 6 Here-and-Now enables them to show a united front.

	SAM HUNT 1+1+4+8+3+5+2	SALLY HUNT 1+1+3+3+7+8+3+5+2
PERSONALITY	6	5
LIFE PATH	6.3.1950 = 6	5.2.1951 = 5
SOUL	4	2
DESTINY	6	6
HERE-AND-NOW	6	6

you would rather paper over the cracks and pretend that everything in the garden is rosy. When a break-up occurs between you and a friend or partner, people may be astonished, so good are you at keeping up appearances. Sometimes this can be very wearing for you, and it could help you to realize that no one will think less of you because you cannot make something work.

To make you feel happy, any partner needs to take your emotions into consideration – you need empathy and support. You also need someone who understands the importance of how things *look*. The most wonderful person in the world will get the cold shoulder from you if they come out looking bedraggled, or behave less than charmingly to your family and friends.

As a lover and a life partner

Wine, roses and being swept off your feet are what life is all about. A big white wedding followed by a lovers' dream in a country cottage, quickly leading to the patter of tiny feet – you are probably a traditionalist at heart, and you want to settle down. It will be very important to you for your partner to get on with your family, but you need to make sure that you also involve your in-laws. Your parents and siblings may wear a path to your front door, but if you value your relationship you need to be very careful that you have private time with your lover, or he or she could feel second best. Sensual and tactile, you find sex blissful as an expression of love, although being friends matters too. Jealousy can be an issue, and it will help if you can bring yourself to talk to a trusted outsider about this so you keep things in perspective – your partner looking at someone else means nothing. All in all, you 'do' relationships brilliantly, so why spoil it?

As a friend

You gather people around you who share your interests, and you probably have several close friends that you rely on for emotional support. Empathic and compassionate, your company can be very soothing. Just sometimes, however, you find the trials and traumas of your

Teaching offers Six the chance to relate helpfully and meaningfully to others.

acquaintances so fascinating that you become more interested in the story than giving sympathy. If you remember not to be a busybody and *never* to judge, you will be the most sought-after companion on the block.

As a business partner

You are an invaluable asset when it comes to creating a good impression. An organized workstation, and a welcoming ambience – you remember everyone's favourite beverage, you buy the cakes and you say the right thing. In any business involving the arts or teaching, you shine. You are best with a dynamic partner who comes up with ideas for you to 'airbrush', and deals with the dirty work.

287

COMPATIBILITY

With 1   Not an easy ride and you may greatly irritate each other, yet there is something that keeps you both coming back for more. This could be a karmic union with deep soul-searching – if you work at it, great things are possible.

With 2   You have a similar outlook on life and from the outside things could look good. Money and possessions are not everything. Don't bottle up your emotions, and get rid of any hidden agendas.

With 3   This is a very creative union and you have lots to offer the world – in fact you could get so caught up in cultural and social projects that you neglect your partnership. Don't.

With 4   It may seem as if you are getting along like a house on fire until you wake up one morning to find the face on the pillow is a stranger's. If you avoid making assumptions and really talk, you will make good progress together.

With 5   You make a lovely couple, but Five could provoke your jealous streak. You need to keep the excitement going in the relationship. Don't give too much too quickly.

With 6   Wonderful for the romance and family that you both probably want. You can create other beautiful things too, but don't be too casual or too hedonistic.

With 7   This could be hard going. You both have different priorities, and obstacles keep cropping up, but with patience you can build something that lasts.

With 8   A very exciting partnership, electric yet potentially stable. Make sure you have lots of projects to work on together. Good communication is key.

With 9   Home and community matter to you both, but for different reasons. Don't question things too deeply and make sure you have plenty of adventures together.

Traditions are important in your relationships if you have a strong element of Six.

Number 7

Your Seven influence can take you one of two ways. You may be hopelessly idealistic to the point where you create a complete fantasy world, in which you and the other party play out fairytale roles against a mythical background. This can work fine as long as the image remains intact. This fantasy world may still be going strong, decades later, long after everyone expected it all to end in tears. Is this self-deception or creative thinking? If it makes you happy, it hardly matters.

The other possibility is almost opposite. You may give nothing away in relationships until you have found out everything that needs to be known, and more, about the other person. This may enhance your tantalizing air of unavailability, or it could mean that partnerships grind to a halt before they have even started because there is no trust. If your counterpart is vulnerable, they may 'jump through hoops' trying to prove their commitment and devotion, but you may still be trawling through bags and pockets and surreptitiously scanning the mobile phone while its owner is in the bathroom. This is an extreme possibility but, if you get anywhere near it, that means you are insecure and you need to

Tips

- Truth is a subtle thing. Remember that you will never get at the truth through poking and prying. Your intuition will tell you much more
- Life and people can never match a dream, but that does not mean dreams have to be discarded. Work at bringing your dreams to Earth, and with everything they mean to you
- Trying to change the other person is doomed to failure. You know that. So change yourself
- Accept that your partner may not truly understand you, but don't compromise on respect

Seven can mean an idealistic dreamer and project an air of mystery.

use your imagination more positively before you wreck everything. Suspicion demeans you, and you are worth much more than that.

When you function well, your spirituality shines through in all your dealings – this shows especially with Seven as your Personality or Here-and-Now Number. Extremely idealistic, you are more than just a dreamer – you actively work to make those dreams real, and with Seven as your Life Path or Destiny Number you may make a special effort in this area. When dreams do become real, there may be a temporary sense of loss, because however wonderful reality may be it can never hold the glamour of fantasy. However, this divine discontent motivates you to seek something even better, and with Seven as your Soul Number you constantly seek enchantment. Your

POWERFUL 7

Adam is Karen's boyfriend. Her 7 Soul is strongly attracted by his powerful 7 combination. He seems to her to be mysterious and deep and she admires his ideals but she doesn't have as much fun with him as her 3 nature might sometimes like, and her flirty behaviour can make him moody.

	ADAM BATEN 1+4+1+4+2+1+2+5+5	KAREN MARKS 2+1+9+5+5+4+1+9+2+1
PERSONALITY	7	7
LIFE PATH	7.11.1987 = 7	3.9.1989 = 7
SOUL	8	7
DESTINY	7	3
HERE-AND-NOW	1	4

combination of extreme sensitivity and dynamism can make you very exciting. Any partner needs to understand that you need space and solitude as well as reassurance that you are valued. They also need to be able to enter your dreams with you or at least never to prick your bubble.

As a lover and a life partner

You may have boundless charisma and the naïvety of a child dressed for a party. You bring to love a combination of extreme vulnerability and blinding insight. Relating to you is never going to be an easy ride. One day you seem to want everything, and be prepared to give everything, and your demands and the heights of your passion may be second to none. The next day you may disappear, either mentally into a world of your own or physically into the next room or the next town. What you need is reassurance that you are truly loved, along with the space to be yourself. Once that is recognized, you can bring both excitement and freedom to your partner, in a relationship that can fulfil all the needs of you both. It is important that you look closely at yourself and think how *you* would feel if someone behaved as you do. Sometimes it may work better for you to have the kind of relationship where you just meet at weekends, because that keeps the thrill going but can also provide you with security. It helps if your partner is the practical one – you supply the ideas and the champagne. If times are hard, you have a fabulous way of creating an image of a better future, as long as worries don't bring you down. Sex can be a mind-blowing fusion of body and soul – or hardly happen at all.

As a friend

You are idealistic about your friends and want to believe the best of them. You like to help them make changes, so you may encourage them to analyse themselves so that they can be stronger (you need to do this delicately). The feeling of belonging to a closed group or secret society appeals to you, and you love the idea that you and your associates may be changing the world in a subtle way.

As a business partner

You need someone down-to-earth, who will sort out practical details, man the workstation and make sure you stop for lunch. You are the creative thinker. You can spot insincerity at a hundred paces and you get a 'feeling' about which deals to go for and whom to trust. You will need time on your own to decide about all of this. A venture that brings about some radical change will be best.

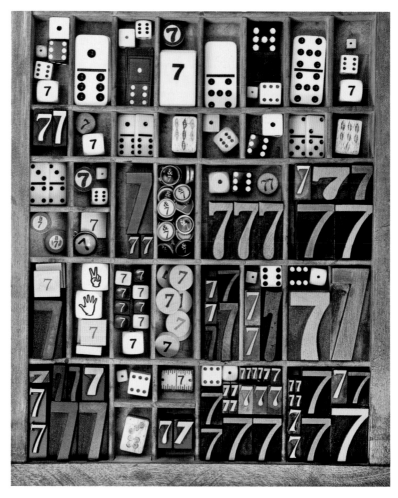

Sevens are complex, never more so than in relationships.

COMPATIBILITY

With 1   Together you can build something very strong, but there could be power struggles. You both need your own space, but make sure you retain emotional closeness.

With 2   You are both vulnerable, but your needs don't dovetail – Two's wish to be 'joined at the hip' drives you crazy. Communication and a little self-sacrifice can bring you happiness.

With 3   The optimism of Three rubs off on you and together you are dynamic. Shared goals bind you, but don't spend too much time apart.

With 4   You complement each other. With tolerance, you could be almost perfect but disagreements could lead to deadlock. Don't slide into shared negativity.

With 5   Very exciting and sexy. Five could make you jealous, so don't be too available and never ask questions; then your air of mystery will always keep them wanting more.

With 6   You both have a vision of perfection, but it is not the same. Scale down your visions and build a life that you can both manage. You will enjoy the security.

With 7   This partnership brings you both out of the shadows and into something really dynamic. You have the power to surprise and excite each other, but don't be too unpredictable.

With 8   Domestic harmony is possible, but you must each have your separate roles. You could find Eight controlling, while they find you spooky. If you both keep a sense of humour, this could be interesting.

With 9   If you share a spiritual or idealistic vision this will work beautifully, and you could be co-explorers. Dogma could divide you if you don't share it – stick with the deeper values.

Number 8

Your Eight influence means that power will be a factor in relationships in some way, and probably in several ways. If you are functioning in a healthy and positive fashion, you will love to have a partner who is potent, and a force to be reckoned with. Of course you will expect respect too, and there may be some lively disagreements that you find exciting and that keep you strongly involved.

If your confidence has been damaged, however, you may need to be the one who always comes out on top, and this could mean that you try to walk all over your partner, or only bond with someone you know is inferior to you or who will collude by being a victim.

As a couple you will feel good if you exercise power, perhaps by running a business together or having influence in the local community – this applies especially with Eight as your Life Path or Destiny Number. With Eight as your Soul Number, money and affection are likely to be bound up together – you may want to feel you have material goods to offer and/or that your partner has the same. This does not mean that you are materialistic (although you may be). The point is rather that money and success are a proof of effectuality, and that is what turns you on. Eight as your Here-and-Now or Personality Number means that you need to thrill your partner – look for adoration and grand passion, and give in return.

Tips

- Never sweep power issues under the carpet. Deal with these openly and your relationship will thrive
- Ensure that your relationship furthers your ambitions or that you are achieving lots together
- You need a partner who makes you feel good about yourself – make sure you reciprocate
- A successful partnership involves really listening to the other party and making an effort to empathize – compatibility cannot be forced

ALL THE EIGHTS

Rob is Jake's boss. His 8 Personality and Here-and-Now numbers mean he comes across as dynamic, forceful and very much the manager. His 3 Soul and Destiny make him seem more human to Jake, but his power-driven approach is tough on Jake's idealistic 9.

	ROB FARLEY 9+6+2+6+1+9+3+5+7	JAKE HUNT 1+1+2+5+8+3+5+2
PERSONALITY	8	3
LIFE PATH	8.6.1963 = 6	3.7.1982 = 3
SOUL	3	9
DESTINY	3	9
HERE-AND-NOW	8	9

You may enjoy teaching your partner to become more powerful or effectual, or you both may derive huge satisfaction from acting together to empower others. Success is important to you in everything you do, and so making a successful partnership matters very much, and you will put a lot into it. Whatever type of partnership you are involved in, you need someone with a strength and personal presence that matches yours, and who can stimulate you, challenge you at times and thoroughly appreciate you.

As a lover and a life partner

Your idea of a great relationship starts with love at first sight, followed by fabulous sex and a strong bond that holds through the ups and downs of life and gives you both support and security. You have a forceful presence and you know how to look good – attracting a good-looking partner should not be hard and this can boost your ego and help you make a stunning impression. However, you need to remember that beauty is only skin deep and you need lots more if you are not to get bored. Despite your practicality you need to be stirred spiritually, and a relationship with karmic undertones will attract you. Between the sheets you like to give a good performance, and dominance games may please you. Out of the bedroom you may welcome a partner who will actually take control of an area of life – maybe your social calendar, or the housework. You have many balls to juggle and you need to be able to trust your partner totally. You cannot abide anything sloppy or unreliable and, if there is a hint of this, you may wrest control back, and rule with an iron hand. This does not make you a control freak, although that is possible. It is more the case that efficiency is important to you because without it you do not achieve so much – and joint accomplishments are the cement that binds you.

As a friend

Small talk has limited appeal – you want to be able to discuss big issues and you don't mind a heated debate. You may alarm quieter or less intense individuals, but those who understand you truly rate your loyalty and dynamism, and of all the numbers to have in your corner Eight is the first choice.

As a business partner

Great as a manager and entrepreneur, you must have a counterpart who will look after the refinements, such as flowers at the workstation. There is not much you cannot handle, but you would rather not handle it alone, and reliable help is invaluable. You need someone who does not mind you bossing them, but refuses to be a punchbag.

Sex can be very important to a forceful eight.

COMPATIBILITY

With 1 This can be a fabulous adventure – you will always respect each other and can do great things together. Although you can both be selfish people, you can bring out the best in each other and reveal deeper parts of your nature.

With 2 Can work fabulously with Two as supportive helpmeet, but if you don't try hard to communicate you could both feel lonely and misunderstood. Two must not get downtrodden, as that will be bad for both of you.

With 3 Interesting and exciting. You fascinate each other and Three keeps you optimistic. Friends may be surprised how well you dovetail, and so may you.

With 4 Everything is so sorted that you are freed up for happy interludes together – you just need to make sure that you have the time and energy to party. Don't take life too seriously.

With 5 You have so much to offer each other but you will need to exercise patience. Hitches are likely. Work at understanding each other, and take things step by step. Five must understand the need to be practical, and Eight must be prepared to adapt.

With 6 Eventful, with lots of shared friends and travel. The pace could be fast, so be careful that you don't lose track of priorities. You may have to deal with more changes than you like, but you can support each other.

With 7 A very happy home and sex life as you each play your complementary roles. Something profound is going on, but neither of you may be quite sure what.

With 8 Power issues are very likely and this could result in withholding and manipulation. Hints won't do – thrash it out face to face and remember that the best part of breaking up is making up.

With 9 What you achieve together is not just about success for you both but has meanings for the wider community. This could be a deep and karmic bond.

Eights may be goal-oriented in relationships.

Nines can be passionate, dramatic and high-minded in love.

Number 9

When you fall in love there is a return to the time of legend. Gods and goddesses walk the Earth and everything is clothed in celestial light. You may be convinced that no one has ever felt quite like this before as the wings of love take you beyond the stratosphere. You like to think that you and your lover can change the world. Being extremely passionate, you want this to be returned, so that you are both swept up in something that is 'bigger than both of us'.

However, you may have strict standards in relationships, and you will want your partner to keep to these, or you may end up preaching at them. If you cannot find a partnership that is 'right', you may decide you were meant to devote your life to other matters.

Nine as your Personality or Here-and-Now Number means that you like to be seen as an exceptional pair. If you are good at something like music or dance, you will love to show off together. Maybe you can support and inspire each other for the betterment of the common cause, but you will also like people to know that you are very much in love; if they are a little envious, so much the better. With Nine as your Soul Number, someone who shares your spirituality can bring you ecstasy.

Tips

- Focus on shared motives, feelings and reactions rather than arguing over points of principle
- Remember the three Cs – creativity, culture and causes. Find elements of each to share with your partner
- Make sacrifices for your partner and enter deeply into their joys
- Sharing your spirituality is essential – don't compromise too much on this

STRONG 9

Here we meet the couple in our original example. Jake has a strongly 9 make-up, so he is very idealistic and has strong standards. Anna finds him hard work at times, but her deep-seeing 7 admires him and their shared 3s ensure they have plenty of fun times together.

	JAKE HUNT 1+1+2+5+8+3+5+2	ANNA MARKS 1+5+5+1+4+1+9+2+1
PERSONALITY	3	8
LIFE PATH	3.7.1982 = 3	8.3.1985 = 7
SOUL	9	3
DESTINY	9	2
HERE-AND-NOW	9	3

Nine as a Life Path or Destiny Number means you will take choosing a partner very seriously. Earnest and idealistic, you want your relationship to be based on the highest standards and the purest emotions and to be of benefit to people other than just you two.

You do your utmost to please your partner, but you rarely become a doormat – mutual respect has to be part of the picture. Debating with your partner will make you feel connected, although if you disagree about really important things it could be a strain on the relationship.

Sharing beliefs is a top priority, but you also like to be with someone who is joyful and as intense about life as you are. You would rather hitch your wagon to a star than settle down in a small house, and you need someone who will enjoy adventuring with you.

As a lover and a life partner

One-night stands are unlikely to appeal and you don't see the point of dating for fun. You are convinced that there is someone for everyone, and you have faith that destiny will bring your soulmate to you. The 'hotline' you seem to have to higher power usually means that your eyes meet across a crowded room and you feel sure that you have been together in a former life – it was 'meant to be'. Once committed, it is essential that you share values and beliefs. You won't want to live in each other's pockets but you need to be on the same journey, and you will delight in each other's achievements and self-development. You may especially like to support your partner in self-awareness and to feel you are both growing as people. Sexually you are lusty, uninhibited and adventurous, but if something does not feel quite right you can be turned off, and you may dislike anything too coarse. You like to feel that the sensual can be raised to a higher level, so you may be interested in Tantric sex, or want your spirituality to be involved in your sexual experiences, which can make for ecstasy but also sometimes for comedy. Luckily, you have a great sense of humour.

As a friend

You like your friends to share your beliefs and you often meet people through being part of the same cause, such as working together for charity. You are extremely idealistic about friendships and like them to be based on truth and loyalty – anything gossipy or two-faced makes you uncomfortable. You will walk through fire for a friend, but sometimes you may split on ideological grounds.

As a business partner

You are great at finding wider scope for your venture and you have terrific imagination. You want your enterprise to be a bit out of the ordinary, and ethics may enter the picture, such as issues of fair trade. Coping with administration is not your forte, and leaving you to scrutinize the 'small print' is courting disaster. You work well with someone who is down-to-earth and can remind you of practicalities.

Nines can be very exact about what they expect in a relationship.

COMPATIBILITY

With 1 Exciting and dynamic, but you may feel you don't really connect. One may seem selfish to you, but somehow that may not matter as you are both going in the same direction with a following wind.

With 2 You feel supported and encouraged but you may also feel that Two does not totally understand you, and cannot quite enter your dreams. Be tolerant.

With 3 Lots of fun and games. Three may seem superficial but you cannot help feeling that anything is possible when you are together. Creative ventures could go especially well for you.

With 4 You are on solid ground and you have to acknowledge it is comfortable, even though you may long to take the brakes off. You need to work at appreciating each other.

With 5 Plenty of discussion, but it often seems as if you have totally different perspectives. Let Five help you with communication and think of all the things you are achieving, rather than criticizing.

With 6 You can be really happy together and it may seem as if Six shares your ideals, although you are more passionate about them. Don't expect too much.

With 7 Both deep and intense, this could be explosive and compelling or spell trouble – or both. Let the relationship bring out the better side of each of you and it could be more romantic than Romeo and Juliet.

With 8 Different ideals, but Eight could show you how to gain the influence you want and bring about some real change. It may feel like destiny is at work – a strongly magnetic tie.

With 9 Lots of things in common if you share the same outlook on life – otherwise you will be on different missions. Don't neglect the physical side of your relationship and make sure you have fun together. Shared adventures will turn you on.

Number 11

If you have a strong element of Eleven in your make-up, then you are certainly going to expect a great deal of relationships. You will be willing to give hugely, but there may be a subtext – you may assume that the utmost in terms of dedication and self-sacrifice is part of the package. Although there may be a selfish element to this, you may also be prepared, quite literally, to die for the one you love.

STRONG 11

David is Ellen's brother-in-law. They share an 11 Soul while David has an 11 Personality. As young adults they were passionate about politics and shared avant-garde views. David pursued this and is now active in the Green Party. Ellen stopped being active when she married David's brother and started a family, but she becomes animated in her brother-in-law's company and calls him her 'soul mate.' Her children feel that Uncle Dave gets Mum on her soap-box.

	ELLEN MARKS 5+3+3+5+5+4+1+9+2+1	DAVID MARKS 4+1+4+9+4+4+1+9+2+1
PERSONALITY	2	11
LIFE PATH	2.9.1953 = 2	11.7.1951 = 7
SOUL	11/2	11/2
DESTINY	2	3
HERE-AND-NOW	3	22/4

This kind of intensity can make for the stuff of myth and cinema, but it can also mean disappointment, because other people simply cannot match your all-or-nothing approach. It will help if you can remember that people are not gods and that thoughtlessness and bad habits are part of all of us. Once you are able to love, warts and all, you are truly capable of experiencing the celestial in relationships.

All of the remarks about Two relationships apply to you, but you are more likely to go to, or to yearn for, extremes. You would love to see yourself and your partner as a duo that can make a significant difference to the world together. Eleven as a Personality Number makes you quite proactive in relationships, doing all you can to make things right. As your Soul Number, Eleven brings big dreams and romantic longing. Destiny and Life Path Elevens could be quite single-minded when it comes to forming a permanent relationship, and when you form one you may like to go on a mission together. Here-and-Now Elevens may need a certain amount of drama in order to feel alive.

As a friend, your strong Eleven makes you dedicated, but you may feel you know best and long to sort out your friends' troubles in order to save them suffering – you need to be careful that this does not backfire, leaving you carrying the can. If you are involved in business, you may run yourself ragged sorting all the details and also driving the operation forward, keeping to the highest ideals. In a committed relationship you may see only your beloved and the things you do together; as long as you both have your space, your capacity for fulfilment is huge.

Tips

- If your head is in the clouds, make sure your feet are on solid earth
- Don't compare your life to an ideal – that can only torment you
- Be aware of how much you are giving and keep some energy for yourself
- Keep a mission that is just your own – discuss it but don't necessarily expect it to be shared

Eleven, as the higher octave of two, can manifest if a partner activates it.

COMPATIBILITY

With 1   You may feel as if you are doing really well, but sometimes you stop and wonder what it all means. There is nothing wrong with having fun, so enjoy.

With 2   You can do fabulous things together, especially if you 'pull out' the Eleven of the other party. Sometimes the minor details will trip you up, so be patient.

With 3   Feelings could run high, but satisfaction may be elusive unless you lower your sights and go with the flow. Change does not mean the end.

With 4   Your ideals can become reality, but only if you are patient. Delight in the smaller things in life, because that is where the divine is found, as you will prove.

With 5   You may want to pin Five down, and they may question you about things you feel should simply be 'known'. This relationship can involve deep issues and may have a compelling quality, so you both learn from it.

With 6   Support and affection can mean you accomplish great things and together you may be influential. Remember that charity begins at home. Interactions with friends and family all go into the cosmic melting pot and bring blessings.

With 7   Great if your ideals are the same, but terrible if you have differing views on life and how it should be lived. There is no one right way and love is the great unifier – emotions may run high. Remind yourself of your priorities.

With 8   You could find yourselves on parallel courses. Eight can help you build your dream as long as you are realistic. If you can tolerate having separate areas, when you get together you will be magic.

With 9   Both of you have big ideas. Lots of highs and lows, slamming doors, tearful phone calls, passionate reunions. Can you last the pace? Keep an open mind and an attitude of exploration – trying to pin things down could prove suffocating.

Together we can make a difference – this is what Eleven believes.

Number 22

Like Eleven, your concept of relationships may be written in capital letters. However, you may find yourself more preoccupied with the practicalities and you may get yourself quite stressed trying to sort everything out. Not only do the feelings have to be celestial, but the material circumstances should match them. So you may want a beautiful love nest, a state-of-the-art car and money in the bank before you feel you have enough to offer, or that you have created a situation that comes up to the mark of your vision.

However, you may be so busy with whatever 'great work' is occupying your thoughts that you may not leave yourself time for relationships. You may find that you are so involved with groups of people, with planning and organizing, that one-to-one partnerships get shelved. It may be hard to relate to you because you may not have the time to devote to more mundane matters.

With Twenty-Two as your Personality Number, you work incredibly hard, never quite feeling you have done enough. Closeness and affection are very important to you, and you need reassurance that you have done well. As a Life Path or Destiny Number, Twenty-Two brings grand schemes, with strong emotions to power them. As your Soul Number, Twenty-Two insists on openness

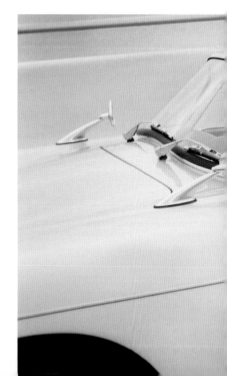

Tips

- Lighten up. Just by having fun you are learning something
- Eternity exists in a moment – not everything has to be lasting
- Let other people take some responsibility
- Pour energy into things you can control and let relationships find their own way, to some extent

22

Twenty-two in love wants material gifts to reflect emotions.

and honesty, needing both emotional commitment and practical security. Twenty-Two as your Here-and-Now Number makes you feel responsible for much in your environment, and you will often take the role of trusty organizer.

With a strong Twenty-Two, all the characteristics of Four are with you, yet amplified and powered by extra emotion.

As a friend you will give the utmost in practical help and you need to be careful not to deplete your own resources and bank balance. In business you have many talents, but you will want to be ethical, and emotional issues may sway you. As a lover you are looking at the long term – you may need to learn to play, to date and flirt, and not to take things so seriously.

DOUBLE 2

The Master Numbers are evident in the interplay between David and his son Frazer. Frazer's 22 Personality expresses itself in his organization of his Dad's campaigns, his Personality adding force to David's Here-and-Now, his Life Path giving focus to David's 11 Personality. When they are occupied in politics and large-scale plans, the 11 and 22 characteristics of their Here-and-Now numbers are relevant, but in a family setting they may revert to 2 and 4.

	FRAZER MARKS 6+9+1+8+5+9+4+1+9+2+1	DAVID MARKS 4+1+4+9+4+4+1+9+2+1
PERSONALITY	22	11
LIFE PATH	22.6.1981 = 11/2	11.7.1951 = 7
SOUL	7	11/2
DESTINY	1	3
HERE-AND-NOW	11/2	22/4

COMPATIBILITY

With 1   This could be hot to handle. One may be too self-absorbed and you may find the unpredictable quality of the relationship upsets and frustrates you. It could be a sexy encounter with a lifetime of new experiences.

With 2   This can work very well, with Two as the loyal helpmeet that gives you support in the background, but sometimes you may feel bogged down by the pettiness of life, so be patient.

With 3   Neither of you may quite understand why you are so strongly attracted, but this can be a compelling, chalk-and-cheese relationship that causes you both to ask deep and meaningful questions, and the right questions are more important than answers.

With 4   If you stimulate the Twenty-Two element in your partner, life will improve materially for you both and your experience will widen. Together you could wield power, and wealth, but avoid complacency and manipulation.

With 5   Both of you will broaden your horizons because of your encounter. Five can show you some resourceful approaches, so don't be too high-minded or stubborn to take advantage.

With 6   Lots of things click, and you both see the need to do something worthwhile with your lives. You may find it easy to act as a unit, but you need to keep discussing things or one day you may find you have separate agendas.

With 7   You may have very distinct approaches but these have an interesting way of dovetailing; when you realize alternatives work, life is richer. You may sense the other's feelings and build a wordless closeness.

With 8   Despite the fact that you both have a serious outlook on life, together you have fun. This relationship can give you both playtime, and effectuality.

With 9   Although your ideals may differ, you may relish the challenge of translating Nine's ideas into reality. Be careful not to demand too much of each other and accept differing priorities and standards.

7: Personal Cycles

You are born with certain numbers but as the years roll on others also come into play. Examining the stage in life you find yourself at, using numerology, can shed light on your past, present and future.

Introduction to Personal Cycles

Although many of the numbers that you have will stay with you for life,
numerology is also a dynamic process. Each year brings its own number-
signature, which influences all of us.

The year 2013 is a 6 year, also composed of the numbers 2 and 13. 2 highlights the millennium and the probability that we are on the road to creating harmony and balance with more self-awareness, after a thousand years of the single-minded tunnel-vision of 1. 13 has a reputation for being unlucky, but it relates to the yearly cycle of the Moon and actually brings spiritual growth, based on the realism of 4 (from 1+3). The 6 year total brings hopes for peace, negotiation and greater understanding between nations as social issues take precedence and disadvantaged countries receive help – although hidden self-interest could be a motivator. Humankind needs to be aware of the forces inherent in these numbers, for when large groups of people are involved, the numbers often operate more primitively, and more negatively. Remember that not all parts of the world have the same method of numbering years. The more you are aware of the *zeitgeist* and in tune with the year number, the more successful you will be.

Of much more individual interest, however, is your own Personal Year Number. This shows the phase you are currently passing through and the changes, issues, challenges and opportunities you can look out for. If your current year number echoes one of your important numbers, especially your Personality or Life Path Number, you will have a special opportunity to develop yourself – but you may also face some crisis of confidence, as you confront what you have achieved to date. Sometimes, during a Personal Year, you may be acutely aware of the things that were important last time round. For instance, if you were given a promotion during a Personal 8 Year, the following Personal 8 Year, which comes 9 years later, may show you how well you have done and bring rewards, or it may herald a complete change, where you question your position.

Some days are luckier than others but you can make the best of them.

Your Personal Year Number

To work out your current Personal Year, simply add the digits of the day and month on which you were born, to the year of your last birthday.

So, if you were born on 14 July 1980, your Life Path Number is:

$$1+4+7+1+9+8+0 = 30, = 3.$$

During February 2013, for instance, your current Personal Year is found by adding:

$$1+4+7+2+0+1+2 = 17, 1+7=8.$$

So your Personal Year Number is 8, until your birthday in 2013, when you will enter your 9 Personal Year.

Year 1

During your Personal Year One, you are likely to make new starts in all manner of respects. This may be in your career, education, relationships or home life. In fact you may take off in a fresh direction in several areas – if you don't, the question is why not? The energies of One demand that you show your independence and originality, and maybe put your blinkers on, for this is not the time to be thinking too much about what other people expect from you (with obvious sensible exceptions).

If you don't move forward, you can have the opposite circumstance of being very stuck; if this happens you will feel enormously frustrated to the point where it can affect your well-being. During a One year, almost any movement will be better than no movement at all, even if it proves to be in the wrong direction. You can always change tack – and it is important to remind yourself of this during a One cycle, because something inside you may be telling you to stick to your guns. You should *not* stick to a course that is taking you nowhere – what you should stick to is your independence. Being able to tell the difference between stubbornness and free thinking is one of the keys to success this year.

A good way to start Personal Year One is to have a massive clear-out. You can begin with the basics, such as your messy

Things to do

- Clear out possessions, jobs, relationships and so on that are past their best and/or not working
- Set clear goals – but be flexible
- Be prepared to change course if necessary
- Have a makeover
- Move house
- Get a new career
- Start a relationship
- Make sure you have time to relax – *this is important*
- Be positive about your achievements and abilities

Aim high during a One year.

cupboards and overloaded computer hard drive. This may not seem like much, but symbolically it is telling you that you are making way for the new. Then you can progress to bigger things that are not working for you, such as your wardrobe, car, home, job and relationships. Certainly, you don't *have* to get rid of all these things – in fact anything that is right for you can now take on a new lease of life. But if the worn-out and unworkable do not bite the dust now they will slow you down and may stymie you totally. Be brave.

What have you been wanting to do for a long time? Although it is best not to take too long mulling this over, don't rush it. Some of your dreams may have been buried without trace through force of circumstance or lack of self-belief, and it is now time to resurrect the ones that could work for you. Avoid taking on too much. One is not a great year for multi-tasking, and, while several projects may be on the go together, they should occupy different areas of your life – for instance, one major new career direction or one relationship.

Don't expect to steam ahead, carrying all before you. During a Personal Year

One there are bound to be some growing pains. This does not mean that you are on the wrong course; 'when the going gets tough, the tough get going', and you are cutting a fresh pathway for yourself. Doubts are common, emotional pain is likely, mental strain is almost inevitable – in fact One years are among the most stressful, so you *must* get your quota of rest and relaxation. Look at your nutrition and exercise, because you need to be strong and healthy for this year. You may feel quite impatient with other people – explain to them what is going on inside you so they understand and realize it won't go on for ever. Once you have gained some momentum (or before, if you feel sure) set yourself long-term goals, but also have short-term ones that you can reach quickly, to give you a sense of achievement. You don't have to achieve all your goals this year; the ones that are right for you can be pursued for many years – you will just take a slightly different approach during other Personal Year cycles.

If you reach the end of your Personal Year One having cleared the way, reached a few small goals and set in motion at least one larger one, you will have used the year to best advantage. This is a really fabulous year for getting somewhere.

Year 2

Your Personal Year Two is about you and the 'Other'. This may be someone with whom you are in a relationship, but it may just as well be you and your achievements and your vision of yourself. While last year, during your One cycle, you were forging a path, now it is time to take a long, hard look at what you are doing, and be objective. You may have to sort out the details arising from decisions you have taken.

It is important to do a little self-analysis, but be careful not to become over-critical of yourself. One of the greatest dangers of this year is that you could go into a negative spiral and virtually undo all that you created last year – don't do it. It is natural to be somewhat less positive and dynamic now, but be constructive.

Personal Year Two is about finding balance. So you may need to consider whether the time you spend at work is offset by your leisure hours, whether you think as much of others as you do of yourself, whether your material concerns are equalled by your spiritual interests, and so on. During a Two year everything has a counterpart, and you may feel you are continually faced with choices. Like the donkey with the two bales of hay, you may feel frozen to the spot at times, dithering between a pair of equally attractive (or unattractive) alternatives until

Relationships are key in a Two year.

you feel quite disempowered. However, rest assured you are learning things about yourself and the world, and one of them may be the need for patience. If you are resourceful you may often find ways of 'having your cake and eating it'. Unless you absolutely have to make a choice, try to avoid it, for at the moment you can see both sides too clearly for this to be easy. But don't let things get to the point where someone else makes the decisions for you – Two years can make you passive and compliant. Being pleasant is one thing, but a pushover is quite another.

Compromise is key now and if you have been involved in disputes, or if your single-mindedness during your One year has damaged friendships, you can now build bridges. Look for common ground, for things that you can do together with someone else and for ways to earn respect through being helpful, supportive and understanding. Friends may start to gravitate towards you for tea and sympathy, and you will be able to draw on your experience to help them. It may sometimes feel as if you are achieving very little apart from pacifying others, but that can be deeply gratifying.

However, Two cycles sometimes signify conflict. If there is some person or organization that has become a thorn in your side, this may now turn into open warfare. During a Two year it can be easy to get locked into a point of view that may have little true value. Don't be stubborn. If you feel you are getting nowhere, ask someone you respect for their candid opinion. Sometimes it takes a wise third party to break the deadlock.

One of the nicest things about a Two cycle is the opportunity to make relationships with other people. These may be firm friendships, associations with colleagues and business partners or a meeting with your soulmate. You should be able to identify with the feelings and viewpoints of others, and this will make you attractive and magnetic. Deep inside, you are looking for someone to complement you, so it is possible that you will be drawn to someone who is opposite to you in many ways. Whatever the case, if you are looking for that special someone, your Personal Year Two should bring you plenty of opportunities to couple up. However, don't panic if you are on your own – Two years can magnify loneliness, but it does not have to last.

By the end of your Two year, you should know yourself better and have formed at least one or two significant associations. Existing relationships should be on a better footing, with greater understanding between you. Partnerships that are truly unworkable are likely to break completely during a Two cycle, as the problems between you become insurmountable. For a marriage that has hit the rocks, Two years are likely to bring divorce, and the necessity for thrashing out who gets what and who does what. During your Two cycle, aim to be placid but not passive, analytical but not negative, practical but also flexible. At the completion of your Two year, you should have greater equilibrium in all respects.

Closeness and companionship come in Two years.

Things to do

- Join a dating agency, if you are looking for love
- Review your work/leisure balance
- Sort out problems in any relationship – consider couple counselling
- Start joint projects or concentrate on activities that require a companion
- Where possible, make peace with people or issues that have been bugging you
- Play Agony Aunt
- Be very honest with yourself
- Read the small print
- Choose well whom or what you serve

Year 3

Having resolved some of the doubts and dilemmas of your Two cycle, your Personal Year Three sees you going from strength to strength. Creativity is the order of the day and any skills and talents you have should reach their finest expression. If you have assumed that you are just another average person, your Three year will show you how you can shine and be unique.

During your Three cycle your creativity may surprise you.

This is a time of achievement. You may not be forging ahead in the way you did during your One cycle, but you will probably get more done and feel more satisfied. Having 'slain your dragons', you can now explore your potential, and this should be a joyful and happy time. You will find your sense of humour is at its

Things to do

- Develop a skill or talent
- Seek out as many opportunities as you can to have a laugh
- Build playtime into your schedule – this is a great year for a major celebration
- Follow up all opportunities
- Start a family
- Create something that you and others admire
- Enjoy works of art, music and shows
- Follow the line of least resistance sometimes, and see where it leads
- Do some things you have always wanted to do

maximum, and that for some reason you are lucky, finding yourself in the right place at the right time. Some things may fall into your lap, but your good fortune is coming mostly from the fact that you are open and relaxed. This makes you more observant. It also makes you more playful – a keynote of the Three cycle – and when we play we tend to discover things about ourselves and the world that can be amazing.

So is it all good news during a Three year? It is true that serendipity is smiling, but don't take things for granted. It could be all too easy to assume that life is a bowl of cherries and you will be able to pick them whenever you want. *'Mañana'* ('tomorrow') could be your motto, as you avoid anything unpleasant or demanding and simply have a great time. Enjoying yourself does have a value because you will recharge your batteries and feel inspired. However, like it or not, things will not always be this pleasant. Opportunities will not always be there for you whenever you can be bothered to take them. During a Three cycle, it is very important to make the most of your assets and opportunities, or at the end of it you could be left out in the cold, not having exploited your gifts, and this could bring you a feeling of intense loss.

During your Three year you will create something new in your life. This could be a literal child, or it could be a 'brain child'. It might be a painting, poetry or something practical like a garment or lots of cooking. The possibilities are endless. What you will want to do, and probably be very able to do, is *make* something that is outside yourself. When you look at it, you may wonder how on earth something so fabulous actually originated from you. In your Three cycle you can be a channel for new life of some description.

If something in life has been holding you back, it may be blasted out of the way during your Three cycle. Self-expression cannot be halted now; if you have been putting up with things that are bugging you, the equilibrium may be upset as you speak your mind. However, this is unlikely to prove traumatic because you probably just cannot quite manage to make a drama out of a crisis (although you may manage a comedy). A Three year is *not* wall-to-wall laughs – in fact, if you have a vision of what you want to accomplish, you will be focused and intense. But it will now be hard to take things quite as seriously as you might at other times and, if your personality contains more 'heavy' numbers such as Four or Eight, your Three year will provide a welcome respite. Make notes on how you feel, keep a scrapbook and take photographs; then you will have plenty to remind you of what it is like to be light-hearted, so you can recreate it.

Do enjoy yourself this year. Is there something you have always wanted to experience? Maybe you long to ride in a hot-air balloon, take a luxury train ride or see shows, exhibitions or spectacles. Now is the time to follow your heart and have a ball – what have you got to lose? 'Life's too short' may be one of your favourite phrases now, even though you may feel immortal. Miss no opportunities and remember that it is usually far better to regret what you *have* done than what you *haven't* done. Three is a year to say yes to life.

Your Three year should bring you fun as well as inspiration.

Year 4

Your life can go in one of two principal ways during your Personal Year Four. If you have used the opportunities of your Three year to express your abilities, your Four year will give you the chance to consolidate these. True, you may find there are some projects that don't work as well as you hoped, and some may have to be scrapped altogether.

There may be hitches and drawbacks, but in general the things that are right for you will endure and take on a more solid foundation. This will ultimately bring you some satisfaction. If, however, you have spent your Three cycle partying, your Four year will bring you up with a jolt as you have to confront the results of your actions – or inaction.

Four is all about building something that lasts. We all know that foundations have to be laid at the basis of any structure, and that can involve lots of digging and dirty work before anything starts to show. Frustrations are bound to be an issue during a Four cycle. You may feel boxed in at all sides, bedevilled by details and continually battling with negatives. Past thoughtlessness may come back to haunt you. What you need is patience, because you will win through in the end. While you may wish you could have done more, what you do will stand the test of time.

Four can seem a very negative year if you don't have very much to build on, or if you have wasted your resources. For instance, if you have got into debt, this could become a major issue with a Four year. You cannot leave those bills under the doormat – somehow you are going to have to deal with the realities of the situation. It may seem as if there is no way out, and you may feel panicky, but actually if you grapple with matters, rather than trying to run away, you will eventually feel very pleased with what you have done and things will become more manageable. So, if life has not been treating you well, or if you have been kidding yourself and others about what you have and do, then Four may seem like the last straw. 'Everything's going wrong!' you may mutter to yourself, but really it is not quite like that. Four will help you confront exactly what is amiss. If not much is right, it is better to go forward knowing where you stand rather than

Patience and attention to detail bring satisfaction in a Four cycle.

nurturing false hopes. By firmly pointing you in the direction of what is actually possible, Four can be your friend.

If you start a relationship in a Four year, it may be one that takes you to your diamond jubilee, but it is likely to be a 'slow burn' rather than 'bells and rockets'. You will have to sort out issues concerning money and where you live sooner rather than later and there may be practical obstacles to overcome, such as distance, working different shifts or other obligations. If you are in a relationship that is not working, now may be the time to tackle a separation or divorce, along with maintenance payments and who is responsible for what. Four is not bad for relationships – far from it. It is just that it firmly removes the rose-tinted spectacles and insists that you work with the practicalities.

Don't be afraid to tackle demanding tasks.

In business, Four is a time to consolidate. Borrowing should be limited, and you will probably find that expansion is slow. If, however, your business is built on solid foundations, this can be an achieving year, where your assets grow. This may not be a great year to start a venture, but working out the nuts and bolts in preparation for your sparky Five cycle is worth doing.

During your Four cycle, you will probably take on greater responsibility. For instance, you may set up home on your own, start providing for children or work hard to keep something you started afloat. You may find that you have taken on too much, and however hard you try you cannot get it right. The lesson here to learn is that you have indeed bitten off more than you can chew. Do your best and learn from your mistakes, so that you don't repeat them. If life is getting you down, you have let your problems overwhelm you, and in fact you are not being realistic. Remember all the good things that have happened to you and are happening to others, everyday, everywhere. Take your first step towards that next goal.

Things to do

- Cut back on any unnecessary expenditure of time or money
- Deal with 'red tape' and administration with patience and thoroughness
- Face up to anything unpleasant you have been avoiding
- Build strong foundations for your ventures
- Sort out your finances
- Develop a workable routine in your personal and professional life
- Avoid making yourself responsible for things that you cannot control, such as the environment – you have enough on your plate
- Organize your home and workstation
- Make sure you eat well, sleep well and get enough rest and relaxation

Year 5

As your Personal Year Five gains momentum, you will find that obstacles disappear and the pace speeds up. You may be bombarded by messages and offers and there will be lots of journeys to take. Most of these will be short, but a longer trip far afield is possible. You can now appreciate all the efforts you made during your Four year, waving a happy goodbye to anything that did not work out. All that may now seem irrelevant, as your priorities change and your horizons widen.

If your Four year did not offer you very much to build on, you may cut your losses and break free. This may be all very well, but remember that, while it might feel good to enjoy yourself for a while, sooner or later you will have to face up to responsibility again. This cycle is certainly about taking a few chances, but not about losing sight of reality.

You may find that inspiring ideas come thick and fast. The challenge may be to pick which ones to develop. One of the worst things that could happen this year is that you procrastinate, flirting with this and that and not giving anything a chance to take root. Most of what pops into your mind will have potential, and almost anything you explore will take you somewhere worthwhile, so take the plunge.

Communication is paramount this year. You may hear a few home truths, but you will quite quickly find these liberating. If you have been suppressing thoughts and feelings for practical purposes, it is likely that everything will spill out now. This could appear temporarily destructive, but very soon you will be moving on and wondering why on earth you put up with

The sky could be the limit in your Five cycle.

Things to do

- Try something new – small things daily, bigger things weekly or monthly, and one or two major new things in the year
- Write a novel, poetry or a blog
- Keep a journal or travelogue
- Make sure you have a well-organized address book
- Keep your mobile phone to hand and consider having a back-up phone in case things go wrong, because you will need to be contactable
- Build a website and/or extend your activity on social networking websites
- Visit places you have never been to
- Speak your mind on important matters
- Start a short course or learn a new skill

so much for so long. Any relationship that has become a burden is unlikely to survive your Five cycle. New relationships are likely, but you will probably find it hard to stay faithful and it may be much better to wait until your Six cycle to tie the knot. A good relationship can now become more exciting as you explore new things together, and you should actively seek to put more impetus into it.

In business, the time is auspicious to take a few risks, but never bet more than you can afford to lose. You should not be too impulsive either – first thoughts are often best, but listen to advice also. You can inject new life into tired ventures because you are thinking unconventionally. You will also be very resourceful – if things don't go as planned, keep your head and you will soon find a way out. Your Five cycle is a good time to go back to school – your receptive brain will be able to learn new approaches.

This is a year full of changes. Just when you think you have got it sussed, something tips the board and the pieces are all over the place again. This year is teaching you to adapt and be flexible. However much the goalposts move, you can score, as long as you trust to your own reactions. Everything around you may be going crazy, but your Five year enables you to find that creative centre within and when all else is unreliable you still can depend on yourself.

Although you may set several things in motion, this may not be a year to commit; that will come later when you have the measure of what is possible. Be an opportunist – don't yearn for the 'good old days' or try to fit anything or anyone into an old format. Even if you don't quite understand what is happening, don't panic. Keep your sense of humour and take things lightly. Five years can be stressful – you may feel wired and tense, with a hundred balls in the air, and in the worst cases Five years can bring you to the verge of a breakdown as it all 'gets too much'. But that is just a matter of how you are looking at things, and the lesson of Five is that 'this too shall pass'. Not that you will be in a rush to complete your Five cycle – the time may seem to fly by, as you are having so much fun and so many new experiences. This could all be very tiring, so, while it may be hard to relax, make sure you play as hard as you work. You could look back on this year as a memorable one, when you really knew what it meant to be alive.

In your Five year you may be inundated with messages and opportunities.

Year 6

After the ups and downs of your Five cycle, you may feel that you deserve some rest and relaxation. Indeed this may come in your Personal Year Six, but you will only be able to benefit truly if you are on an even keel emotionally. This may be hard to achieve during a Six year, because you will be very aware of anything that is not harmonious and balanced, and you may be hypersensitive.

Whatever may not be quite right in your relationships or in your extended family is now likely to become an issue. At worst, you may become very upset about this, but at least it promises some measure of solution, as issues come out into the open and can be resolved. You may wear your heart on your sleeve this year, but that is no bad thing. People have to know how you feel – otherwise how can they take it into consideration?

This could be a year of passion and tantrums, as you try to make your significant relationships as close to perfect as possible. People being what they are, this is bound to cause you some traumas, but you can tease out the issues and make some significant changes. A relationship that really is not satisfying you may now have to go because you need to be able to seek something better. However, the opposite is also possible.

You may resolutely put your blinkers on and insist that everything is fine when everyone else can see that it is not. You may also glamorize your involvements, turning them into a kind of fantasy. For instance, your lover might be selfish and demanding but you could attribute that to overwhelming passion. Or you could see yourself as the princess who has been rescued by the knight in shining armour, when what has really happened is that you have surrendered control of your life. Get back to reality. This year offers you a great opportunity to find fulfilment and true romance, but not if you fool yourself.

Family matters are likely to predominate this year. A close relative may be ill and needing your care; or there may be important events such as engagements,

Your Six year can be productive and fulfilling.

Things to do

- Tackle practical projects that will make your home more attractive
- Hold family celebrations and reunions
- Develop your skills as a cook or gardener
- Get in the habit of listening to music, or something similar, each day
- Face family issues – family therapy may be an option
- Seek romance – if you are single, try singles' clubs and holidays, or speed dating; if in a relationship, make time for candlelit dinners
- Get involved in a local charity or project and/or get closer to your neighbours
- Have cosmetic surgery or a complete makeover
- Look up lost relatives and old schoolfriends

Peace is essential for you in your Six years.

weddings and births. Funerals are also possible, and while these may be sad they will also offer opportunities to meet up again with old friends and distant family members, and your sense of being part of a community will be strengthened and enriched.

The 'global family' may also preoccupy you, and you may be quite worried about the things you hear on the news. There may be an impulse to 'mother the world', or you may be especially concerned about world events that could impinge upon your nearest and dearest. Try not to be anxious. There really is no point worrying about things you cannot control, and you are doing more good than you realize by thinking positively and spreading love and compassion. You may possibly become involved in local concerns such as 'neighbourhood watch', or a local charity that takes meals to old people or cares for bereaved children. You will gain considerable fulfilment from something like this and you will also enjoy it in a less noble fashion because you will be the first with all the gossip. There is no harm having some fun but don't be a busybody or tell tales because you will feel awful if you are found out, and it could have far-reaching consequences.

This year you need to be careful not to over-commit. If you are in business you will need to be careful that your better nature is not exploited. You may find it especially hard to say no to anyone needy, but if you don't maintain sensible boundaries you could run yourself ragged and be little good to anyone, especially yourself. This could then lead to compensatory behaviour that won't enhance your well-being, such as comfort eating, 'retail therapy' or even something more extreme such as turning to alcohol or drugs.

Ask yourself what there is in your life that you would like to make more beautiful. This year you should concentrate on something artistic, and by the end of your Six cycle there should be something in your life that will give you abiding pleasure. Develop your creativity and make sure that you have regular times when you can be peaceful and serene. If you spend a half an hour a day listening to calming music or meditating, this will help you return to your centre and re-emerge into the world ready to bring to it, and yourself, greater blessings.

Year 7

Last year you may have been awash with emotion. In your Personal Year Seven, you will probably question everything you feel, and that everyone else feels too. Changes are going on within you now, and you may not feel comfortable about what you perceive. However, it is very important that you are honest with yourself, because unless things come to the surface they cannot transform, and you could then be motivated by unconscious promptings that are not in your best interests.

This would be a good year to go into deep psychotherapy, if that interests you. You should take note of your dreams and also trust your gut instincts. Yes, intuition can be wrong, but so can logic. The more you trust your inner promptings, the stronger they will grow. You may like to develop your psychic abilities through Tarot, astrology or similar, or you may like to attend a séance, or study to be a medium yourself. Now is the time to step far out of your comfort zone, and have the courage to explore new territory.

Relationships that started, or were cemented last year, may now go through a testing period. Possibly you may question your choice and you may even wonder if you want a relationship at all. You may watch your partner closely, and even become suspicious – make sure you keep this in perspective. You must be careful to keep things in proportion – be patient, give things time and don't wear your heart on your sleeve. However, don't expect people to read your mind. You need to explain yourself and, if you are not quite sure what is going on inside you, at least say that. For instance, if you sometimes doubt your love for your partner, it would be asking for trouble to say 'I'm not sure I really love you', but it would also be a mistake to be moody and silent. It would be far better to explain that you are going through a confusing time and need to sort yourself out. Make sure that you have plenty of personal space; time on your own is essential and you should explain this to your partner.

You will now be evaluating what you have done during the last seven years, and you will almost certainly find something to criticize. Don't be too hard on yourself.

Deep matters may be your concern in a Seven year.

Now you are searching for a deeper understanding and the person you are in the present is a product of all the lessons you have learned – nothing has been a waste of time. You may feel anxious about a lot of things; some of these will be real and others imaginary. The most important thing is that you understand the difference. Grasp the nettle and change the things that can be changed. As for the others, you must now learn to use your imagination positively. You may begin to find that your thoughts manifest, and what you see in your mind's eye actually comes about. Don't be scared. If you concentrate on what you want and really visualize it coming into your life, it can happen. If you master this trick of creative thinking, this could be one of your most successful years to date.

Skeletons could tumble out of cupboards this year. For instance, a family secret about a legacy or someone's true parentage might be revealed. There may

Things to do

- Start a course and further your education
- Develop your intuition in any way that appeals
- Take note of your dreams
- Investigate your family tree
- Work at understanding yourself more deeply
- Meditate, and have time alone
- Learn to focus your imagination on what you want – hypnotherapy may help with this
- Change your image if something different appeals
- Question your life and your priorities, but avoid sudden decisions and dramatic actions

be some shocks, but their impact is likely to be felt more on your perception of reality, rather than in practical terms. Make sure you don't exaggerate information and events. This year may teach you that change is the only constant. However, the French have a saying *Plus ça change, plus c'est la même chose* ('the more things change, the more they remain the same'), and it could be a comfort to remember this. Be prepared to shift your priorities – many things don't matter nearly as much as people think they do, and this cycle may prove this to you.

You may feel very conscious of what you don't know, so do something about it. If possible go back to college, study through distance learning or sign up for an evening class. Knowledge for its own sake is key, rather than mastering a new skill, but follow what appeals. You may have an urge to change your lifestyle – for instance, if you have always been quite formal and restrained, you may now want a more alternative image. You could feel like selling up and hitting the road in a caravan. Consider anything, but do nothing on impulse. It will take a while to find out where your true future lies.

Focusing your imagination and talents is a great way to use the Seven vibe.

Year 8

After the uncertainties and introspection of last year, your Personal Year Eight feels more dynamic. There may be a sensation of getting caught up in things that are out of your control and certainly you should 'go with the flow'. This does not mean that you will be totally powerless. The trick is to understand the prevailing trends and to work with them.

Choose your battles – some are not worth fighting and some you cannot win. It will be much better to be realistic and to turn things to your advantage rather than try to stop the inevitable. Pragmatism will put you in a strong position, but if you insist on your own way, no matter what, you could suffer badly.

Don't be surprised if issues from the past that you thought were dead and buried resurface in a slightly different form. There may be a feeling of 'karma', and you may have lessons to learn. The sooner you learn them, however, the quicker you will be able to move on. This does not all have to be challenging. Eight is not the easiest vibration, but it does bring some huge rewards.

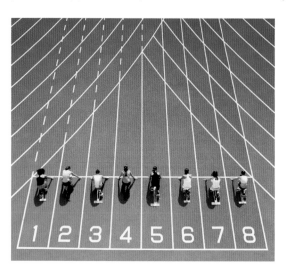

Put your efforts where they count in an Eight year.

If you have some large-scale schemes, your Eight cycle can be the time to put them into practice. You should have sorted out the groundwork during your Seven cycle, and you know who you are and where you stand. There is a danger that you could over-commit, so remember that there are only 24 hours in a day. This is a year for hard work and considerable achievement, but if you overstretch yourself you risk losing everything and that is one lesson you could do without. Avoid getting into debt, and be careful about relying on others. You will probably be reticent in this respect, but someone who is a clever talker and promises some fantastic business opportunity could get past your defences. You need a challenge and something major to go after, so something in you may want to believe there is a promising opening. Don't suspend disbelief because you are impatient to get to grips with something new; you should have fine-tuned your intuition during your Seven cycle, so don't forget to listen to it.

Power will be a factor during your Eight cycle. You may have to cope with bullying or with some person or organization that wants to control you. You may have to think carefully about what is going on because it may not be obvious, and if this is the case it could be difficult for you to regain mastery without appearing to be bossy yourself. You may need to be cunning, but whatever the case it is important that you are master of your own destiny; it may be better to take the chance of appearing uncooperative or controlling yourself rather than risk becoming a puppet, which would be a very sad expression of the potential of your Eight year.

If you are in a relationship, you may now choose to start a venture together. Having come through some soul-searching last year, you should now be able to move forward and accomplish things. You may have to sort out who controls what, and there may be power struggles and manipulation, but you can work through these. This is a good year to start a business, either in partnership or alone, and there is the potential for making a great deal of money, if you remain sensible.

You can enhance your status this year, and you may want to show this off. By all means indulge yourself in a few status symbols – you will enjoy it as long as you really can afford it. If funds are tight, you can still make an impression if you are clever; for instance, you could scour the charity shops for designer labels. However, you will feel much better if there

You may have more influence in your Eight cycle.

is substance behind the impression you are creating, and you will get a huge thrill if you pass a test, such as your driving test, or achieve promotion. This year you should try for any promotion that appeals and make sure you always look your best, because you never know when it will be your turn in the spotlight. At the end of this year, with a lot of graft, a little luck and a good measure of common sense, you should be in a better position financially and materially than you were before.

Things to do

- Start a business
- Put maximum effort into something that inspires you
- Apply for promotion
- Always look your best and make a good impression
- Cultivate influential people, but be sincere
- Invest in status symbols that are within your means
- Put in for a test or exam
- Train in a skill that is applicable to your business or creative venture

Year 9

Hopefully you feel you consolidated a few things last year, because in your Personal Year Nine it may be harder to focus. It is not that you feel confused, exactly, but some matters that appeared very urgent will now seem to lose their intensity. You may wonder why you wanted what you thought you wanted, and it may seem as if you are searching, but you are not sure for what. The worst thing you could do would be to force the issue.

Try to be patient with yourself – what you need right now is an open mind and the willingness to change if and when that seems right. To 'hold the uncertainty' is your mission this year, and to have faith that you will find a new direction.

Some things will come to an end, and these may be things that you value and/or thought would be with you for ever. Wave them goodbye and move on – if they go they were never yours anyway. Any person or thing that truly belongs with you will remain, and you may come to see them from a new and more vital perspective. Your life is going through a transformation, and in some respects a breaking down, in preparation for the new build-up that will commence with your forthcoming One cycle. You may feel in limbo – some affairs that you thought were settled may drag on, and no matter what you do you cannot bring them to a

conclusion. For instance, you may have decided to move in with a new partner but for some reason you cannot sell your house, or a new job may have been promised but the post is not actually vacant. Don't despair or run away with the idea that 'it was not meant to be'. Probably everything will work out fine but, whether you realize this or not, these delays are teaching you something and giving you the opportunity for reflection. Try to take each day as it comes, live for the present and relax.

As the year progresses, realizations may dawn on you and you may become wiser or more knowledgeable. A few things may fall into place; for instance, some events in the past that seemed random in nature could now form a pattern. You may

Fulfil your Nine urge to travel and experience life or you will find yourself frustrated.

Things to do

- Travel as widely as you can, soaking up experience
- If you cannot travel physically, be an 'armchair traveller'
- Explore and develop your spirituality
- Become involved in a charity
- Express yourself artistically in as crazy a fashion as you like
- Embark on a 'self-help' programme, through reading, with a trained life coach or in an encounter group
- Think about what is not serving you positively; don't struggle to hold on – be brave and let it go
- Start writing a novel, or at least write down your thoughts for they are likely to be profound
- Deepen your education – be curious
- Make *carpe diem* ('seize the day') your motto

be drawn to a religion or spiritual discipline. Certainly it will be a good thing if you develop your spirituality or your thoughts about the place of humanity in the Universe.

You may also find yourself involved in doing good works, possibly for your local community or for a charity. Something more radical may appeal, and if you feel your life in general is not adding up to much you may decide to live abroad, travel the world and/or get involved with ethnic causes. The spirit of this is distinct from the enterprise and decisiveness that might be behind such a venture in a One year; during a Nine cycle you are searching, exploring and letting go. You may even 'let go' literally and go off to join a commune, sell up and take to the road in a caravan, or join a monastery. Seclusion will definitely benefit you and you should try to get to know yourself better, and change any psychological patterns that are not helping you.

During your Nine cycle you may have a certain world-weary air, and it may seem as if nothing really inspires you. Don't panic – this will come back. However, other people may view you as having an aura of experience and wisdom, and you may find that they come to you for advice and help. There may be a temptation to give away too much now, so be careful and don't fall for hard-luck stories. It is fine to give the benefit of your knowledge, but be aware that 'advice is a dangerous gift, even from the wise to the wise' (J R R Tolkein, *Lord of the Rings*). What you say now could come back to haunt you later, and what does not seem to matter very much could become crucial. The greatest wisdom of all could be to support and encourage friends on their own path and keep personal opinions to yourself.

Inspiration can come to you during this cycle. If you are involved in anything creative and artistic, a new light may dawn and you may find you are doing amazing work. This could be because you have become detached from concerns like profit or conformity. However, during your Nine year you will like to make an impression. You will be uplifted by the respect you receive, and this will carry you forward into an exciting fresh start.

Spiritual insights may dawn during your Nine year.

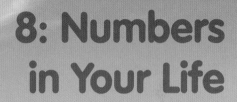

8: Numbers in Your Life

Different ages and situations all have their special number-signature. Examine the numbers all around you – use the space in the back of the book to mark them all down and review them.

Your Age

In addition to the strong influence of your Personal Year cycle (see pages 318–319), the rhythms of life also fluctuate with your age. Each time you gain a year you move along in your cycle – for instance when you are 30 you are influenced by the number Three, and when you are 31 you move on to the influence of Four, and so forth. This can be considered alongside your Personal Year cycle.

This may seem complicated at first, but then life is complex, and no single number is going to be the sole influence on you at any one time. It may help to write down the qualities and lessons of any number that particularly affects you, or which really strikes a chord, so you can concentrate on developing the positive traits. Always follow your intuition and use what feels helpful.

In addition, your nine-year cycles give a very strong background influence, which colours your life experience, and understanding them can be helpful, making it easier to put life trends into context. Growing older is often thought of in negative ways, but numerology also highlights the positive qualities of any age, and these can be developed.

Numbers are with us from the very start of our lives.

First 9-year cycle, Age 0–9

You are influenced by One, and your individuality is forming. You are learning who you are and how and when it is appropriate to assert yourself. Through this nine-year cycle you experience each of the numbers at their purest. Until the age of one, a baby is fused with its mother and through her with the collective of humanity. Still 'trailing clouds of glory' the little one has traces of the Infinite, represented by Zero. Around the age of one, the infant learns to walk and to strike off on their own. Around the age of two, relationships with others are formed and the child becomes more conscious of 'me' and 'not me' – this can cause crisis, as in 'the terrible twos'. At three, you learn to be creative, and play becomes more dynamic, inventive and fun-filled. From the age of four the challenges of school come as more demands are made on you and you have to cope with the 'real' world, outside home.

At age five, communication and education are gaining momentum, and you learn to read and write. At age six, the physical cycles of learning are complete – you probably become more sociable, able to help around the home and to be an active family

Education may be avidly soaked up at age five.

member. Age seven is regarded by some religions as 'the age of reason' when you can know right from wrong – basically this means that you can think and reason now. Childhood fantasy may be left behind or, if you have been encouraged, your intuitions will become clearer. At eight, you meet the challenges of the world more squarely, deciding on your ambitions and consolidating your views of life. Nine marks the last year of the first cycle, with an evaluation of knowledge and a letting go, before moving on to the second cycle, with its accompanying change of perspective.

Second 9-year cycle, Age 10–18
During the teen years, you are developing independence and energetically exploring your individuality. Under the influence of One, this can be a very lonely time, as you struggle with new feelings, believing you are the only one experiencing them. You drive forward in life, maybe unsure of where you are going, but taking increasing responsibility for yourself. This is, however, the second age cycle, and the Two influence means that you experiment with relationships quite intensely. Numerology helps to explain all these strange new feelings and reassure

During your teens the two influence is strongly felt.

you that things will change. When you reach the age of 18, in many countries you will be deemed to be an 'adult'.

Third 9-year cycle, Age 19–27
The overriding Two influence of these years sees you exploring relationships, breaking up, making up and developing a sense of what it means to be a couple. It is important now to learn to compromise. You will also form lasting friendships, for instance at university, as you are able to choose companions more freely and connect with kindred spirits. It is important to use this decade to do this, as it could be a long time before you experience this level of freedom again. Many people now form a committed relationship and/or get married, leaving the nest to express the Two energies by becoming nurturers in their own right. However, this is the third age cycle and the Three effect makes you very sociable, creative and eager for life.

Fourth 9-year cycle, Age 28–36
Four looks for solid achievement and towards the end of your 20s you may experience a crisis, as you evaluate what you have done and realize the world may be bigger than you thought. Keep your head – you have plenty of time. The Three influence in your 30s stimulates your creativity, and your need to express yourself more widely. Career changes

are likely and relationships that were motivated largely by the need to be a couple may now end, if they cannot adapt to your evolving personality – if the relationship is not right, move on.

Fifth 9-year cycle, Age 37–45

This is the classic era of the 'mid-life crisis', which occurs around the age of 40. The Four influence brings you to look at exactly what you have achieved, and for many people this is not enough. There may be a rather panicky feeling as you strive to do all sorts of things, but you should stay calm. You have more time than you think. During your 40s you want consolidation, but this is your fifth cycle and Five is the vibration of change.

Sixth 9-year cycle, Age 46–54

If you have children, your family will now be a dynamic entity. Grandchildren may be born. You may also become more involved in the community. Your parents will be approaching the age at which they need looking after. Consolidation is around, in the lingering Four effect, and with your 50s Five brings change into a dynamic new perspective. You may now have more time to communicate with old friends and to begin new activities – you want fresh stimulation, as you may have more freedom. You should embrace this and make 'use it or lose it' your motto.

Seventh 9-year cycle, Age 55–63

As you move towards your 60s, extended family becomes more important. Older relatives may die, and those remaining may draw closer. Home and neighbours figure more strongly as you think about retirement. The Seven influence brings increasing wisdom and reflection, but 60 is now 'the new 40', and the Six effect strengthens a wish to retain youth and beauty, and could result in cosmetic surgery, fitness classes and so on. You may also want to improve your home and/or garden, or maybe learn something artistic such as painting or sculpture. Nurturing yourself is key.

Eighth 9-year cycle, Age 64–72

If you have now retired, fresh goals will be especially motivating and you may feel influential and determined, with the Eight influence. Moving into your 70s also intensifies the wisdom and analysis of Seven. You may feel there is much you just 'know', and no one is going to fool you. Keep your mind sharp by re-educating yourself. If you draw on the balance and harmony of the lingering Six element, to look after your health, you will be a force to be reckoned with.

During your seventies you can develop instinctual wisdom.

Ninth 9-Year cycle, Age 73–81

This is a culmination, and with the deep-seeing quality of Seven and the wide experience of Nine you should be wise and mellow, able to give sound advice from your experience. Avoid being self-righteous (Nine) or remote (Seven). There is no need to settle into your rocking chair – the up-and-coming Eight influence means you need a challenge, and can wield a lot of power.

Tenth 9-year cycle, Age 82–90

As a matriarch or patriarch, the Eight effect gives you plenty of authority which you should use constructively. Don't tyrannize younger relatives or make them feel guilty – use your experience and wisdom to support and encourage. The return of the One influence may signal a second childhood, but equally it can mean increased independence of mind. This may be a decade of increasing loneliness as contemporaries die, but the lesson is to relate more to younger people.

Eleventh 9-year cycle, Age 91–99

There may be little left to experience as the strong Nine element brings a wide perspective and you may feel very in touch with the whole of humanity and the richness of human experience. Your own youth may seem to have been only yesterday, as you realize that so many things are so closely linked, and our lives are just a blink of an eye in the face of eternity. You will now command respect – live up to this. The Eleven/Two effect brings heightened sensitivity, so you will need peace and will be especially responsive and creative in the field of the arts.

In your eighties you may experience the power of Eight in a very special way.

Car Numbers

Your car number is one of the most important numbers in your life. It relates obviously to the way you travel, the smoothness with which you can run your errands, and your safety. No numbers are 'dangerous', so don't be alarmed. But it is worthwhile noting how well your car number harmonizes with your own numbers, especially your Personality, Life Path and Soul Numbers, because often when we get behind the wheel we revert to a more instinctual self.

There are three numbers that affect your car.

Let us use W55 6DP as an example.

First is the overall number – you arrive at this by totalling the digits and the corresponding letter values (see page 101):

$5+5+5+6+4+7=32,$
$3+2=5.$

Second is the total of the numbers only:

$5+5+6=16, 1+6=7.$

Third is the total of the letters only:

$5+4+7=16, 1+6=7.$

The numbers are the most obvious and reflect the way other drivers see you. The total of the letters reflects the purposes and types of journey, while the overall number – the most important – tells you about the identity of the car. Of course, the car is an inanimate object and does not have a 'personality'. But everything that is created has its own unique vibration, and the numbers pinned to your car have a frequency. If you are not happy with this, you can buy your own personalized number plate, which may change your luck.

In a traffic jam amuse yourself analyzing the numbers of the car in front. Numerology is fun!

1 Very single-minded, this relates to a motorist who may not have much time for ditherers and slow drivers. Always on a mission, your driving is probably very efficient and your concentration good, but be careful that this number does not put you under stress. Play relaxing music and make yourself think about the things you have achieved already.

2 This number influences you to think about other drivers a little too much. You may be a considerate driver, but worrying about the person coming up behind you can make you nervous. You may often be involved in ferrying a friend or family member around; you should remember to think of your own interests and not get too tired.

3 Driving is fun and you can enjoy the sense of movement – you may go out a lot for entertainment. It may suit this car to be customized, or flamboyant in some way, making other drivers take notice. Then you can give them a smile, to make the day go more happily for everyone. While driving you may get creative

367

inspiration, so keep a notebook or dictaphone with you to record this when you stop.

4 You probably own a well-maintained car, for you practicality is paramount, and you have a strong sense of the importance of getting from A to B. This car is good for carrying shopping, DIY equipment and anything useful, as well as for routine journeys. Try not to worry too much about keeping it clean. You

his car too seriously and
won't put you in danger –
g relaxed can bring safety.

ηptation here is to do other
ə you drive. Make sure that you
have a hands-free mobile
phone, because you are
sure to be tempted to
gossip when behind the
wheel. Sometimes you
could get irritable while
driving, at other times you
will be happily distracted
by a million thoughts or
lively music. Like Three, you
should have a notepad or
dictaphone handy to pull
over and record your ideas.
Don't forget to concentrate
on driving safely, however.

6 Great for a family car,
going on outings or doing
anything that is connected
to the community. You will
want the seating to be
comfy – a seven-seater is
great with this number as
you can pile in more

Other road users may
experience another driver
as cooperative or difficult.

people. You may also find you are
involved in charity works – it is a good
number for the helping professions.
Soothing music will help as you drive.

7 There is a risk that you could be
distracted and go off into a world of your
own – you may even find that you end up
at the wrong destination because your
mind was on higher things. A sat-nav
device will really help you. However, the
great thing is that you often find the right
place by intuition. Driving can take you to
other worlds, as you enjoy the scenery.

8 It is very important for you to drive
well, and you may be tempted to try to
teach others how to do it – for example,
pointedly going back into the inner lane
on motorways every time you overtake,
which can be dangerous. Calm down.
While in the car you will need to be in
contact with people that matter – as with
Five, a hands-free phone is essential for
you, and all the technology to make you
efficient. You will feel best in this car if the
model is impressive.

9 Driving may seem a waste of time,
but you can make it count by playing CDs
that teach you something. It is important
for this car to be as environment-friendly
as possible. Giving lifts and car-sharing
will make it all feel more worthwhile.

House numbers

The number of your house is a very important number – it is literally 'where you live'. Add the digits of your house number until you have reduced them to a single digit: for example, 28=2+8=1, 103=1+0+3=4. If your house has no number then turn the letters of the name into digits and add them/reduce them as for your name.

1 This house is a stimulating environment for creativity and enterprise. It could suit a dynamic person working from home, or anyone with strength and originality. People who are determined, individualistic and self-motivated thrive here, and find success. There is an upbeat atmosphere, with something interesting always going on.

AVOID trying too hard to make everyone share and mingle. Each person needs their own space in this house, because it encourages independence.

2 The atmosphere here is welcoming and sociable, and the kettle is always on the boil. This house suits polite, charming people who enjoy entertaining. Cooperation is the key, and care needs to be taken not to overlook anything. A minimalist décor suits the peaceful ambience. It is a great place to have meetings, for agreement is likely.

AVOID clutter. It will make people irritable and spoil the mood, because this house only functions well when everything is harmonious. Ugly ornaments are *out*.

3 This is a cheerful home that encourages celebration. It is good for artistic and creative people, and always seems to be full of sunshine. It is especially favourable for large families, and easily creates a romantic ambience, as long as everyone is honest and faithful. This house is comfortable and beautiful, and brings out the extravagant side of its inhabitants.

AVOID trying to be too serious, or very tidy. To do this would be to stifle the light-hearted atmosphere of this house.

4 Common sense is the word in this house. It favours a practical approach, and calls for all family members to do their bit. Routine is encouraged and security fostered. It may be a good home

The number on the outside can reflect conditions on the inside.

from which to build up a business. Respect from neighbours and the community is readily achievable here. **AVOID** leaving doors and windows open and flapping, even when you are at home, because this house functions best when it is very secure and organized. For the same reason, keep up with any maintenance and gardening that needs doing.

5 This is a hive of activity, where routines go out of the window and the furniture is constantly rearranged. The pace can be crazy, with lots of comings and goings and a host of interesting things being done at any given time. Children thrive here, and so do pets. This is a modern home that welcomes progressive views. **AVOID** trying to be too quiet – it just is not what this house is meant for. So, for solitude, go for a walk. Unless a grandparent is very lively, having them move in is a bad idea.

6 This home creates an ambience of 'belonging', with family ties and a sense of community being all-important. Traditions are respected

If you live in a flat, you will also be influenced by the number of the building. This Six flat is great for happy families.

and much care is devoted to bringing up children. Cooperation and pulling together are the keynote. Caring and sharing are encouraged, together with a sense of responsibility for the neighbourhood. There is always a welcome on the mat. **AVOID** neglecting décor and housework, and don't get rid of heirlooms or things that the children make, because a sense of family, dignity and continuity are essential to this house.

7 Solitude and study are favoured by this home, which creates a calm, deep atmosphere that is good for meditating. Anyone who seeks wisdom finds shelter here, and strength and independence are favoured. This home can be a haven of peace for those disillusioned with the world, who like their own company, and want a chance to probe below the surface of life.

AVOID trying to have the 'party of the year' in this house, because its air of peacefulness could manifest as a wet blanket. Gaudy colours, barking dogs and loud music won't feel right, for the same reason.

This One house is great for people who like their own company.

8 This home is a good 'base' for people with responsibility and a position to uphold in the community. Nothing but the best will do – this home likes to create an impression. Usually this is a very well-run home, and a thriving business can be built up here, especially if it is community-oriented. It favours confident, controlled people who know what they want.

AVOID tatty curtains, tacky ornaments and rubbish in the front garden. Don't let external paintwork deteriorate, because this house gives greatest security when it is in perfect shape.

9 Here is the place for broad-mindedness, compassion and tolerance. Waifs, strays and differing ethnic backgrounds are welcome, and this home calls for high-mindedness and deep understanding. It is a house that expands mental and physical horizons, welcoming lovers of the arts and all types of beauty, and encouraging idealism and integrity.

AVOID turning away surprise guests (unless impossible), because this house feels happiest with a humanitarian approach and plenty going on. Don't run a business here, unless it is artistic or charitable – the atmosphere is too bohemian for it to succeed.

Telephone Numbers

Your telephone number is very important to your life and your identity, because it is a number that you are giving out all the time. People continually use it to get in contact with you, so subconsciously associating it with you. Often your number will be memorized, and reeled off in connection with you. If you don't feel in harmony with your number, or find that you are not getting the calls you want, it could be worth considering changing it on purpose.

There are several numbers that may be associated with you. Your mobile phone number is probably the most important. You arrive at it the same way as all other numerology formulas – by adding the digits and reducing to a single digit. However, notice also the individual digits because if one of them repeats several times it can colour the final number. Another is your fixed-line number. Again, add the digits until they reduce. For out-of-area calls, include your dialling code – this may bring in a different influence.

If you work in an office, your extension number is important – take that on its own and add the digits as usual, until they reduce. Your extension number shows how you are regarded and how you function within the organization.

Interpreting the numbers

1 You probably find that you are left on your own to handle things for much of the time. Where is the help when you need it? Of course, it may suit you to work alone, especially if 1 is also your Life Path or Personality Number. If this is your extension number, make sure that you don't take on too much, and cover your back. If it is your home or mobile number, you may receive demanding calls, or one-sided calls. It could be good for getting your point over, but is not ideal for expansive social chatting.

2 You are probably always being asked for advice. People see you as the one who will sort things out and you may find that you say 'yes' without really meaning to at times. If it is your extension number, be careful that not too much is expected of

Your telephone number buzzer with its own special vibe.

you – you cannot be a solution to everyone's problems. If it is your home or mobile number, expect heart-to-hearts and a massive bill.

3 Getting involved in jokes and banter is easy – this is a good number for sales and anything creative. However, it might be hard to get things straight and after a great conversation you may find you come off the phone with very little settled. Remember that the 'feel-good factor' is not everything, especially if it is your extension at work. As a home or mobile number it brings lots of fun and dates.

4 If this is your extension, practical solutions are key – it will be hard to fob people off without a direct answer and you may feel that you are always being pinned down. It is very important to say what you mean and always keep your commitments. As a home or mobile number, this favours getting things straight, making arrangements, and so on, but not chit-chat.

5 Arguments are possible with this number, but if you can keep your cool you can certainly get results. You may find that

If things aren't going smoothly a change of number would help.

379

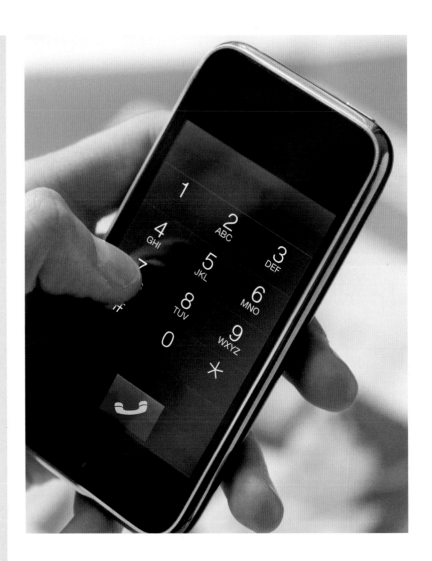

you or your callers get impatient, so keep to the point. Ideas may come down the line thick and fast, so make sure you make notes before they leave your head. If it is your extension number, you will have to think on your feet. As a home or mobile number, it brings lots of repartee, and is great for anything journalistic, or to keep in contact with a wide circle.

6 This is a good number for creativity, and for soothing any caller who is stressed. But you may be tempted to call home a lot if this is your extension number. Long, pleasant chats are likely, with a wealth of descriptions and gossip, but it may be hard to bring things to a conclusion or reach decisions. You may find you get involved in community work, or a telephone tree.

7 This is not a talkative number, and for some reason which you cannot explain you may feel reluctant to answer the phone at all. Misunderstandings are likely, and you may not be able to hear properly. Don't be afraid to ask callers to repeat what they have said so you get it right, especially if this is your extension number.

If you are investigating something, this number is favourable, and you may get strong intuitions while on the line.

8 This is a great number if you are the boss. You may find that you come across as quite authoritative with this extension, always doing the organizing and saying who goes where. You are probably still on the line when everyone has left the office – don't work too hard. If this is your home or mobile number, you will probably sound important and a force to be reckoned with, so use this well, and be firm but also polite.

9 If you are calling on this extension number, it may be hard to keep to the point. It is all too easy to go off at a tangent. You will get some fantastic ideas from your callers, but they may not be the ones you were looking for. This is a great number, however, if you are arranging trips and holidays. You may find you are giving out important information, or that you hear things that really change your life. A superficial chat with a colleague could easily become a deep philosophical discussion when made on this number.

Your telephone number is as important as your extension number.

Lucky Numbers

Most people want to know what their 'lucky number' is, so that they can use it to become more successful in life. The truth of the matter is that your lucky numbers are actually those that turn up in your Five Formulas. Those numbers describe your individuality. If you work at understanding them, personal insight and developing yourself, then you will naturally maximize your luck because you will be in harmony with yourself.

Research has shown that people who are relaxed, outgoing and fun-loving tend to attract 'good luck'. 'Luck' comes from being in tune with your surroundings – it is the playful, happy-go-lucky soul who is likely to spot the money lying on the ground, while the anxious, preoccupied person may be too caught up in their own troublesome thoughts to notice. More laid-back people also tend to listen to their intuition. Thinking positive is the greatest luck-attracter of all, and you can be relaxed and optimistic whatever your numbers may be.

Life-changing strokes of luck, such as winning the lottery, do seem to come from the hand of Fate. However, research has also shown that most people, when they win huge sums, are no happier a year or so later than they were before chance made them multi-millionaires. So when you seek 'luck', be careful what you are wishing for. The greatest luck of all is a feeling of contentment.

If you are determined to use numbers to get lucky, then it is a good idea to use the numbers in your formulas. The ancient numerologists taught that the number of your name was the most potent, for the vibration of the sound is created every time it is pronounced. In fact, it is probably better to use the formula that is most relevant in whatever situation you are seeking your stroke of luck. For instance, if you are buying raffle tickets with your friends, choose the ones that add up to your Here-and-Now Number, because that is the vibration that is going to surround you throughout the event as your mates chat to you. If you are doing the lottery, it is best to include your Personality and Life Path Numbers.

Relax and tune into your lucky vibes.

If entering a draw for a family holiday, the luckiest number might be your Destiny Number. Making a bid to win a stay at a retreat, a yoga course or similar might be most suited to your Soul Number. Think about exactly what is involved, before choosing your number.

If your lucky number is Six, for instance, then to improve your fortunes you can try bringing this number increasingly into your life. Where possible, postpone matters of importance until days that add up to Six – the 6th, 15th and 24th (be wary, however, of putting numerology before

Maximize your chances using numerology.

Pick a winner with number wisdom.

cities, towns and villages all have their numerological identity. Paris, capital of romance and passion, is a Nine, while tolerant London is a Two. Bear in mind also the Soul Number formed by the vowels in the name of the town, for Paris has a Soul Number of One, reflecting a certain egotism and opportunity for self-expression, while London's Soul Number is Three, promising fun along with wonderful theatres and art galleries.

If you feel that nothing is going right for you, then the solution could be to change your name, because this will, in time, have an undeniable effect on your life. In fact, it may have a very dramatic and swift effect, as I discovered when I altered my

common sense – if something needs doing urgently don't wait for a Six day). If you go to the races, try to back a horse that carries the number Six, and if the name of the horse adds up to Six then you have an even better chance. Choose to live in a town that also adds up to Six, for

name from variety-loving wordsmith Teresa (Five), to impulsive and romantic Tess (Nine). One of the most well-known name changes was that of Napoleon Buonaparte to Napoleon Bonaparte. The first name, containing the 'u', adds up to One in the Hebrew system (see page 13) – the number of assertion, ambition and leadership. In the modern system, it adds up to Seven – less obviously appropriate maybe, but the intuition and almost magical ability to mould events characteristic of a positively functioning Seven could be seen in charismatic Napoleon. Without the 'u', in both systems the name reduces to Four, which is much more low-key, prone to doing things the hard way and finding life burdensome. A negatively functioning Four influence overshadowed the Emperor's latter years and his eventual defeat. So, if you want to change your name, think carefully about it.

Finally, a lucky number may reveal itself to you in life. For instance, you may find that a certain number repeats in house names, birthdays, etc. You will probably find that this fits in with one of your Formulas, but, if not, Fate is still trying to tell you something. Listen, and follow where it leads.

From the highest to the lowest, numbers exert their subtle influences.

Notes

Notes

Glossary

Aspects – the angles the planets form in the astrological horoscope.

Birthchart – this is a map of the Heavens, particularly the planets and certain important astronomical points, drawn up for the exact time of a person's birth.

Chaldean – refers to the Mesopotamian region, considered the cradle of civilisation.

Correspondence – Subtle, magical links between the manifest world and the abstract. Venus corresponds with love and affection, lapis lazuli, jade, doves etc. Rituals use correspondences, such as rose petals and a pink candle in a spell.

Esoteric – this means 'hidden' and refers to knowledge not obvious, often arrived at through inspiration and/ or initiation.

Pythagoras – a Greek Mathematician and philosopher c. 570 BC, from Samos.

Feng Shui – 'wind-water', an ancient Chinese system of arranging living space with harmony and balance

Horary astrology – a purely divinatory rather than natal form. A question is posed, a chart of the Heavens drawn up for the moment of the question and then the chart is interpreted to find an answer.

Lo Shu – 'magic square' with nine smaller squares in three rows each containing a number. Each row amounts to 15 when added up. Symbol of stability.

Manifests – comes into physical being.

Major Arcana – these are the 22 Tarot 'trumps' or picture symbols which carry powerful archetypal meanings.

Menorah – a 7 or 9-branched Jewish candle-holder linked to the Tree of Life.

Minor Arcana – the 56 remaining cards in the Tarot, divided into 4 suits, Pentacles, Cups, Rods and Swords

Resonance – vibrational power, influence and connection

Pa Kua – this is a balanced design formed from the I Ching symbols, used to bring harmony and good luck.

Qabalah – ancient mystic Jewish doctrine.

Sephiroth – (singular sephirah) stages/ attributes in the process of manifestation, from the Divine to the Material. They appear on the Tree of Life and are ten in number, although 'Da-ath, The Hidden One' may be considered an eleventh.

Tarot – ancient card pack used for divination. There are many forms of Tarot but carry essentially similar meanings.

Taoism – a philosophical and mystical tradition of East Asia c 2,500 years old

Tree of Life/Ets Chayyim – a diagram of manifestation starting with purest spirit through to densest matter. The ten sephiroth appear on the Tree of Life.

Vibration – all of existence is composed of vibration. Differing vibrations have a different character and some may harmonise better than others.

Index

Figures in *italics* indicate captions.

Acknowledgements

akg-images Electa 62

Alamy Chuck Eckert 384; doughoughton 367; Fancy 356-7; Gianni Dagli Orti/Art Archive 12, 57; Ian Shaw 258; Imagebroker 61; incamerastock 316-7; jvphoto 81; Mary Evans Picture Library 93, 95; North Wind Picture Archives 7; Photononstop 64; superclic 319; Tetra Images 275; The Print Collector 35

Corbis 22-3, 184; Adam Woolfitt 45; Adie Bush/cultura 42-3; Angelo Cavalli 157; Ant Strack 38-9; Bernd Vogel 96-7, 186-7; Bettmann 109, 129, 176; Bob Thomas 138; Boyd Jaynes/Transtock 245; Brigitte Sporrer/cultura 173, 181; Darren Kemper 121; David Papazian 167; David Vintiner 371; Eric Audras/PhotoAlto 250-51; Flint 164; Jack Hollingsworth 197; Juice Images 174-5; Jutta Klee 240-41; Michael Haegele 193; Moodboard 191; Newmann 58-9; Nicky Niederstrasser 117; Nicole Hill/Rubberball 2; Ocean 98, 105, 114, 279; Patricia Curi 246; Paul Burns/cultura 30-31; Paul Seheult/Eye Ubiquitous 68-9; Paul Taylor 194; PBNJ Productions/Blend Images 33, 106-7, 144-5, 147; Per Winbladh 26-7; Rachel Frank 113; Radius Images 148; Rafal Strzechowski/ZenShui 183; Randy Faris 167-8; Reg Charity 134; S Hammid 302; Simon Marcus 135-6; Stephen Vidler/Eurasia Press 73; Steve Hix/Somos Images 158;

Sylvain Sonnet 54-5; Tadashi Ono/amanaimages 223; Tammy Hanratty 131; Tetra Images 242-3; Tim Kiusalaas 73-4; Tim Pannell 205, 328, 339; VStock LLC/Klaus Tiedge/Tetra Images 210; Whisson/Jordan 155; Zero Creatives/cultura 50-51

Fotolia Aaron Amat 150; Africa Studio 215; Antony McAulay 49; by-studio 103; Dean Pennala 8; ft2010 70; Hanik 377; iofoto 125; javarman 71; jjayo 142; johnnychaos 372-3; jonnysek 77; julien 221; MartiniDry 217; Monkey Business 286-7; photo-dave 385; Rafa Irusta 386-7; sitriel 110; Vision Images 249; WavebreakMediaMicro 333; yanlev 16-17; Yuri Arcurs 179, 206, 235, 268-9, 290, 334

Getty Images 189; Alexandre Fundone 201; Altrendo 324, 345; Amy Neunsinger 161; Antonio M Rosario 306; Bambu Productions 202; Bertrand Guay/AFP 163; Brand X Pictures 383; Chris Ryan 342; Daly and Newton 298; Daryl Benson 294; Dave Shafer 289; Donna Day 265; Echo 347; Fuse 232-3, 374; Henrik Sorensen 364; ImageSource 46-7; James Oliver 348; James Whitaker 380; Jill Chen 341; Kevin Winter 141; kkgas 378-9; Lew Robertson 231; Martin Riedl 122; Michael Blann 282; Michael Hitoshi 52; Mike Harrington 363; Nicole Morgenthau 354; Paul Bradbury 257; Paul Viant 330; PhotoAlto/Laurence Mouton 360;

PhotoAlto/Sigrid Olsson 133; Photodisc 126-7; R Nelson 277; ranplett 66; Richard Nolan-Neylan 24; Roger Viollet 119; Ryan Harvey Photography 219; Ryan McVay 336; Salva Lopez Photography 270; Simon Potter 321; Stefano Lunardi 170; Stephen Simpson 359; Stuart O'Sullivan 322-3; Tim Kitchen 326-7; Visuals Unlimited Inc/Wim van Egmond 29; William James Warren 153; Yuri Arcurs 100

Glow Images Foodcollection 225; Image Source/Kalle Singer 236; Mikael Andersson 368; Photosindia.com 227; Tao Images 78

Masterfile Marc Vaughn 312-3

Octopus Publishing Group 218, 220, 222, 224, 226, 228, 230

Reuters Kai Pfaffenbach 21

Rex Features Sipa Press 198

Scala Pierpont Morgan Library/Art Resource 36

Science Photo Library Royal Astronomical Society 34

Thinkstock 301; Creatas 82; George Doyle 350-51, 358; Hemera 19, 208, 229; iStockphoto 83, 84-5, 214; John Foxx 10-11; Jupiterimages 212-3, 353; Medioimages/Photodisc 311; Stockbyte 238, 262

TopFoto Charles Walker 41